angelina jolie
the biography

angelina jolie
the biography

rhona mercer

JOHN BLAKE

Published by John Blake Publishing Ltd,
3 Bramber Court, 2 Bramber Road,
London W14 9PB, England

www.blake.co.uk

First published in hardback in 2007

ISBN: 978-1-84454-365-6

British Library Cataloguing-in-Publication Data:

A catalogue record for this book is available from the British Library.

Design by www.envydesign.co.uk

Printed in Great Britain by Creative Print and Design (Wales)

1 3 5 7 9 10 8 6 4 2

Papers used by John Blake Publishing are natural, recyclable products made from
wood grown in sustainable forests. The manufacturing processes conform to the
environmental regulations of the country of origin.

contents

chapter 1

in the beginning…

'I always live for the moment. Don't like to build plans
for the future. Tomorrow evening everything may change – my life,
my image, people around me, my occupation… Otherwise,
it would be boring to live.' *Angelina Jolie*

Angelina Jolie has grabbed headlines since bursting on to the Hollywood scene over ten years ago and the stunningly beautiful actress remains a constant source of fascination to her millions of fans across the globe. Over the years, we've watched a rebellious, depressed and self-destructive teenager mature into a contented, settled and sophisticated mother of three, and her personal journey has been absorbing to watch. As one of the most open and honest stars of her generation, it's no surprise that Jolie's controversial personal life has garnered far more interest than any film she's ever made, and – love her or loathe her – you could certainly never accuse the actress of being bland.

Born in Los Angeles, California, on 4 June 1975, to actor parents, Angelina Jolie Voight's life was unconventional from the start. Jon Voight married little-known French-Canadian actress Marcheline Bertrand in 1971, and their first child, son James Haven, was born in 1973. But, by the time Bertrand was pregnant with Angelina, their second child, their marriage was already in crisis. It's thought Bertrand rapidly grew tired of Voight's womanising ways – and, sure enough, he soon fell in love with the actress Stacey Pickren, whom he met on the set of the film *Coming Home* (which won him a Best Actor Oscar), and he left his family for her. By the time Angelina was one, her parents had separated.

For the first few years after the split, Marcheline and the children remained in LA and Voight saw his kids regularly, but in 1982 Bertrand moved Angelina and her brother to Sneden's Landing, which was an hour away from Manhattan, because the smog in LA was affecting her health.

Although Angelina has said, 'I never remember a time when I needed my father and he wasn't there,' and that she was 'never angry' with him for leaving, the pair would go on to have an extremely strained, complex and volatile relationship.

For his part, Voight once observed, 'She was a baby when we were divorced, so it surprised me when she said it affected her as severely as it did.'

According to one of Angelina's kindergarten teachers, who doesn't want to be named, Voight was very much a hands-on dad: 'Her father was always picking up her and her brother. He was always around. I don't know if they had a good relationship, all I know is that he did the fatherly thing.' And Jon's parenting skills didn't just extend to the school run. According to the same source, 'He came to sports day. He came to the school. They lived in Palisades, where all the big stars like Al Pacino lived. Angelina was just a little kid, cute, you know. She was always pretty.'

Although the pair haven't spoken since their very public falling out in 2003 – when Voight told the press that his daughter had 'serious emotional problems' – it's clear that, as a child, Angelina was very much a daddy's girl. According to Voight, 'When Marcheline and I broke up, I sat Angie down and asked her what kind of girl she thought her father should be with. She thought about it for a while and then said, "Well, Daddy, maybe me, because I love you more than anything in the world."'

Voight was no less smitten with his daughter and, in an interview they did together in 2002, Voight described to Angelina the moment she was born: 'You don't remember it, but, when you emerged from your mother's womb, I picked you up, held you in my hand and looked at your face. You had your finger by the side of your cheek, and you looked very, very wise, like my old best friend. I started to tell you how your mom and I were so happy to have you here, and

3

that we were going to take great care of you and watch for all those signs of who you were and how we could help you achieve all that wonderful potential God gave you. I made that pledge and everyone in the room started crying. But we weren't crying; we were rapt in each other's gaze.'

After his ex-wife and children had relocated to New York, he confessed that he missed them very much: 'Angie is a real comedienne and Jamie is so grown up,' he revealed at the time. Keen to involve the children in his life even though he no longer lived with them, Voight gave his daughter her first acting role in 1982, casting her as Tosh in *Lookin' to Get Out*, a film about two New York gamblers that he co-wrote and starred in. Keeping it in the family, Voight also gave his ex-wife Marcheline the part of 'girl in jeep' and the role of Rusty went to his then girlfriend, Stacey Pickren.

Keen for his children to see what had been keeping their father busy, Voight often took them to screenings of his latest films including *The Champ*, in which he played an ex-boxer who tries to raise his son single-handedly. 'It was a little hard for them,' Voight observed shortly afterwards, in 1979. 'They both started weeping. The last scene was very unsettling. I had to take them in my arms and explain that Daddy was just acting – that he wasn't dead, that he was still here with them. You see, it is not my intention to walk away from my responsibilities. But I'm also realistic. I know that Marcheline may get married again and that another man will come into their lives.'

Similarly, when their father took them to see *Table for Five* in 1983, James and Angelina found it difficult to separate fiction from reality. The film was a study of children living through a divorce and, according to Voight, 'They found it deeply moving and knew that in some ways the film represents me and my deep feelings about needing to be close to them.'

Voight himself had enjoyed a very close-knit family unit while growing up in Yonkers, New York, with his parents Elmer and Barbara and brothers Barry and James Wesley. (James would later go on to change his name to Chip Taylor and become a legendary songwriter, penning such classics as 'Wild Thing' and 'Angel Of The Morning'.) In many ways, he was keen to be the perfect family man himself, but something kept stopping him. In an interview a year after divorcing Marcheline, he admitted, 'I loved the idea of kids running into their parents' room and jumping into bed with them. But I've never been too sure of myself in terms of words like "husband".'

Chip Taylor admitted in a 2004 interview that Jon had never really recovered from the decision to leave his family: 'Jon was married to a lovely lady [Marcheline]. I don't know why it didn't work, but he fell in love with another girl and ran off with her. That didn't work either and he probably looks back and feels immensely guilty about what he did. He tried his hardest to be a good father, but I don't think he was comfortable in his own skin being a father.'

Angelina has in the past defended this attitude, saying, 'My father is the perfect example of an artist who couldn't be married. He had the perfect family, but there's something about that that's very scary for him.' As her own relationships would go on to prove, the apple clearly hadn't fallen far from the tree.

When Jon left his wife, his career was at an all-time high. He had shot to fame in 1969 playing Joe Buck, a male prostitute in *Midnight Cowboy*, and went on to win an Oscar for his portrayal of Luke Martin, the wheelchair-bound Vietnam veteran in *Coming Home* in 1978. Although Angelina would later go on to benefit from her father's Hollywood connections and knowledge of acting, the attention he received from fans was unwelcome as far as she was concerned. Voight admitted in an interview that his kids were 'growing up in the shadow of my mythology and they need special care because of that. I was having dinner with the kids recently and a man began approaching us. He was apologising from 15 yards away, saying, "Oh, I'm so sorry to bother you... but you look so like... Are you?" My daughter Angie, who wasn't feeling well that night, looked up and said, "Oh, God, not this again." And of course the man just about fell to pieces.'

Despite the upheaval caused by her nomadic childhood, Angelina was a joyful child. She delighted in the Disney film *Dumbo* (she has said that she cried when he found he was able to fly), had a crush on Mr Spock from *Star Trek* and loved to play dress-up with her much-loved older brother James. 'I used to wear costumes all the time,' she recalled in 2001. 'I used to love those plastic high heels.'

The fact that they moved around so much as children meant that Angelina felt like she never had a permanent base and she has said of this time, 'I always dreamed of having an attic of things that I could go back and look at.'

She and her brother leaned on each other for support from the moment she was born and were never short of finding ways to amuse themselves. From as young as five, Angelina would dress up in her mum's clothes, put on some make-up and perform shows while her brother filmed her. This collaboration would continue up until their teens, with Angelina starring in all five of the student films James made while studying at the USC School of Cinema, one of which won him the George Lucas award for directing.

As long as she's been famous, Angelina Jolie has been synonymous with sex. So it comes as no surprise that at kindergarten she became a member of a group named the Kissy Girls. Recalling her first experience of seducing the opposite sex, Angelina admitted, 'I grew up very aware of my emotions. I was very sexual in kindergarten and I created the Kissy Girls. We would chase boys around and kiss them a lot – it involved giving them lovebites – and they would scream. Then a few of the boys stopped and started taking their clothes off and I got into trouble a lot.' So much trouble, in fact, that her parents had to be called to the school to discuss their daughter's rebellious behaviour. Needless to say, the Kissy Girls were no more after this point.

Not that Angelina was much of a girlie girl at heart. While most children beg their parents for a puppy or a kitten, Angelina was more than happy with her pet lizard, Vladimir, and a pet snake named Harry Dean Stanton after the actor. She once said in an interview, 'While other girls wanted to be ballet dancers, I kind of wanted to be a vampire.' Other girls would write the name of their crush on to their pencil cases, but Angelina busied herself with drawings of old people's faces, nude women, mouths screaming and barbed wire stretched across people's eyes.

It wasn't long before her ambition to be a vampire was overtaken by an even stronger desire: to be a funeral director. Her maternal grandfather died when Angelina was nine years old and his funeral would prove to be quite fascinating for the impressionable young girl. Most girls her age would be overwhelmed by the occasion and scared of death, but not Jolie. She was far too preoccupied with how funerals should be conducted to be scared. 'My mother's father died when I was nine. He was a wonderful, spirited man, but his funeral was horrible. Everyone was hysterical. I thought funerals should be a celebration of life rather than a room full of upset people. I'm not scared of death, which makes people think I'm dark, when in fact I'm positive.' She said that she was 'very drawn to some things that are tradition and that are roots. I think that may be why I focused on funerals.' It was after the death of her grandfather that Jolie started to wear black. She even went as far as taking walks in graveyards and reading books on the art of embalming and mortuary science. 'There is something in death that is comforting,' she once reflected. 'The thought that you could die tomorrow frees you to appreciate life now.'

When she was ten, Angelina recalled that her life 'started not to be fun' and, after Marcheline moved her children back to LA, her daughter's rebellious streak grew stronger. In fact, kissing boys in kindergarten seemed positively tame compared with what was to come. She has said of this time, 'I always thought I was sane, but didn't know if I'd be comfortable living in this world. As a child I contemplated suicide a lot – not because I was unhappy, but because I didn't feel useful. I had insomnia and was up all night with a mind that wouldn't stop.'

Angelina has said that she spent much of her childhood 'staring out of my window thinking there was somewhere I could finally be grounded and happy. I belonged somewhere else.' This feeling was probably never stronger than when she enrolled at Beverly Hills High, the most glamorous and affluent school in LA. Her fellow classmates were rich, beautiful and spoiled; Jolie couldn't have been more different. For a start, despite her dad's Hollywood status, there wasn't much money flying around when she was growing up. Voight has always been notoriously fussy when it comes to choosing film roles and rejected several big roles because he didn't feel they were right for him; he famously turned down the lead role in *Love Story*, despite being offered 10 per cent of the profits.

Voight prided himself on the fact that he didn't spoil his children, stating in 1979, 'I have tried to bring up my children to realise the value of money. Because I don't have a swimming pool, when we want to swim we have to get permission to use somebody's pool. I'm aware of the value of things and I want my children to be too.'

Angelina's family lived relatively modestly compared to her peers and, instead of flexing her dad's plastic on Rodeo Drive, the actress bought most of her clothes in charity shops – Aaardvark's in Pasadena being one of her favourite haunts. Like most teenage girls, she also had several hang-ups about her appearance and was teased regularly for having braces, wearing glasses and for being so skinny. Although her bee-stung lips are now one of her most outstanding features, she learned the hard way that anything that made you different at a tender age could only be a bad thing. As if to cultivate her reputation as an outsider, Jolie was also prone to dyeing her hair and permanently wearing black, her favourite colour.

Many of Angelina's glamorous classmates did modelling and, in an attempt to make some extra cash, Jolie tried to get in on the act, despite thinking she looked like a muppet. Although it is hard to believe now, given that she is often referred to as one of the most beautiful women in the world, Angelina initially failed miserably in the competitive profession and was told by agents that she was 'too short, too scarred, too fat, too everything'. The scars that the agents used as an excuse not to hire her were from her self-harming, something that Jolie began at the age of 14 in an attempt to break free from her teenage frustrations. Angelina has since admitted that, 'Thirteen, fourteen – that was a bad time. Yeah, very.' So bad, in fact, that she remembers 'not wanting to be around any more'. Although she has never condoned her behaviour, Angelina has been very open about this phase, reflecting, 'I went through a period when I felt trapped, cutting myself because it felt like I was releasing something. It was honest.' This need to 'feel' had always been one of Jolie's preoccupations, and the actress has admitted that, as far back as childhood, she only liked to be touched in a certain way. 'I don't like when I am lightly touched,' she confesses. 'You see, I like [it] when I am grasped and held tightly, if someone strives not to let me go, and if I am not touched in a proper way, I hate such touching. It's like the handshake – I don't like a light one. If you want to shake my hand, shake properly.'

Jolie certainly knew what she wanted in terms of physical contact with her first boyfriend – and, as we will discover, the consequences were often little short of life-threatening.

Like many children who come from a broken home, Angelina was expert at manipulating her parents, who were competing with each other to be the main influence in her life. When the family moved back to LA, it meant that Voight got to see his kids on Tuesdays, Thursdays and every weekend. Voight admitted in an interview in 1987 that, even at the age of 12, his daughter knew how to wrap him round her little finger. 'She'll spin 45 minutes' homework into maybe an hour and a half, because of her reminiscences and teasing, and then she'll make a game of it. I'm delighted I spend this time with her. We just giggle and shout and we become a bit of a pest to Jamie, whose nature is quite the opposite.' Voight may sound like the smitten father at this stage, but the actor was also aware of Angelina's potential to rebel. In 1987, he described his daughter as 'quite striking, and perhaps a bit more like me – which may be unsettling to her – because she has quick wit, she's very imaginative and very active, she must be doing something continually and I delight in her. She's a bit of a wise guy at this stage – with me she definitely is! Ever since she was a baby she wouldn't let you help her, even with her ABCs. She'd say, "No! I do it. I do it." That's the way she is.'

Unfortunately, by the time she'd hit her teens, Angelina was taking her 'wise guy' act too far and went off the rails completely.

If Angelina didn't get on with her fellow pupils at Beverly Hills High, the teachers were just as alien to her. Undoubtedly at a loss as how to deal with her, they enlisted the help of a psychotherapist. 'They enrolled... everybody whose parents were divorced,' says Jolie of this period. 'One psychotherapist used to say that it was our "units" who were guilty of everything. It seemed to her that we, poor children, would never be able to adapt to life. I was assuring her that I had adapted in a nice way, but for some reason she wanted it to be the other way. After all, I thought out some fairy tale for her – oh how glad she was of it! Since then, I don't believe in psychotherapy.'

Voight shares his daughter's view on the effect divorce has on children, saying, 'It's easy to blame any problems children have on a divorce. But you have to ask yourself if they would arise anyway.'

While Angelina had her say about these sessions, so did the teachers, and in one of her references following these sessions she was described as 'unrestrained' and 'inclined to antisocial psychopathy'. Typically, Jolie was undeterred by this label, admitting frankly, 'Since childhood I was called a sociopath.' (Ironically, she would go on to play one in *Girl, Interrupted* – and it would win her an Oscar.)

Whatever company she was keeping, it's clear from her old school mate Jean Robinson that she wasn't too popular with the other girls in her year. In fact, her reputation as a man-eater dates back to way before she was famous. 'When she was fourteen at Beverly Hills High School, she was stealing boys who were seventeen,' recalls Jean. 'Once they were panting after her, she'd walk away. It was all about the chase.' And according to Jean, it wasn't just the boys

13

Angelina preyed upon. 'The same happened with girls. Angie could seduce you into thinking she was your best friend and then not speak to you again. That kind of cruelty is common, but Angelina was devastatingly good about it.'

Jean also had this to say of Angelina's lack of wealth: 'She lived in an apartment on the wrong side of Beverly Hills, not where the really rich people live. She was deliberately different and didn't want anything to do with the rich kids. She had a serious thing with knives. All kinds of knives – penknives, kitchen knives. She would just whip one out and start playing with it.'

In terms of Angelina being an outcast, Jean explains that 'Beverly Hills was so straight in the early Nineties, everybody was into fitting in and getting good grades. The dress was neat, very expensive preppy clothes. The place to hang out and shop was the Beverly Center, an enormous shopping mall in West Hollywood, or Rodeo Drive for girls with daddy's credit card. Angie wanted no part of that. She hung on Sunset Strip at the punk-rock clubs and shopped at the punk stores on Melrose.'

Jolie herself admits, 'I was that punk in school. I didn't feel clean and, like, pretty. And I always felt interesting or odd or dark ... I'd be in my black boots and my ripped jeans and my old jacket and I felt more comfortable like that. I wasn't gonna pretend to be the smart, clean, centred girl. I could understand the darker things, the more moody things, the more emotional things.'

Of Jolie's penchant for the goth look, Jean comments, 'She was into leather, torn jeans, nasty boots with stiletto heels. Kids were scared of her, the teachers were as well. I don't think there had ever been anybody quite like her at Beverly Hills High.'

While she was clearly looked down upon for daring to be different, this shock factor was likely to have pleased the rebellious Angelina more than acceptance ever would have.

In retrospect, her refusal to conform to Beverly Hills fashion etiquette is something that perhaps should have been admired rather than scorned, but it's clear that her peers were scared of this girl who didn't take social boundaries remotely seriously. Jean says of Jolie's therapy sessions: 'She went there, like, three times a week. She was like, "I'm off to therapy", like it was maths or science. It didn't change her a bit. I think the therapist needed therapy by the time they were done.'

Not all of Angelina's contemporaries were so unforgiving. One, in particular, remembers a more insecure side of her personality. 'I'm not saying she wasn't wild. She was. But she also had a kind of vulnerability and a lot of pain. I think she was deeply hurt by the break-up of her parents and the fact her dad moved on with his life and, for the most part, left her behind. He would occasionally show up and take her out. They went to the Oscars one year. But she wanted a full-time dad, not an Oscars date. It hurt her and made her put on as tough a front as possible so as not to show the pain.'

Perhaps most revealing of all, the same source goes on to talk about Jolie's deep-rooted ambition. 'She was very smart and, in her own way, disciplined. She got into acting very quickly and successfully by 15 or 16. She always said she wanted not to follow in her dad's footsteps but to outdo him, which she did.'

Her uncle, Chip Taylor, could also see straight through his niece's rebellious ways. 'Angie was always the kind of kid that would like to think she was tough,' he says. 'I never looked at her as a tough kid because I've been around real punk kids and she was like a kid from Hollywood doing a little performance in her biker clothes.'

Conforming was clearly very low on Angelina's list of priorities and it's no surprise that her first serious boyfriend didn't exactly fit into the high-school-jock mould. 'She could do just about anything she wanted as a teenager,' says Jean. 'When she was 14, she fell for a punk rocker who was about 16. He was wild too.'

Rather than banning her daughter from seeing this guy, and potentially pushing her daughter away, Bertrand clearly thought the best way to deal with the situation was to keep an eye on it, and so she allowed Angelina to move him into the family home. Angelina said, 'I lost my virginity when I was 14. We were in my bedroom, in my environment, where I was most comfortable and I wasn't in danger. I was very young but kids are doing a lot of weird things these days and they're getting very promiscuous. We lived together for two years with my mom, so I wasn't sneaking around. Unlike other girls, I wasn't partying and hanging out on the street.'

She may not have been sneaking around, but, according to school friend Jean, Angelina's behaviour still left a lot to be desired. 'It was a pretty strange living arrangement, but her mum made the best of it. Angelina dyed her hair purple and had piercings. She was a complete terror. She and her boyfriend went over to the rougher areas to punk clubs, staying out until all hours. That's when she started losing interest in school completely.'

Angelina has since defended her decision to be so serious with someone so young, saying, 'Are you ever emotionally developed enough to be involved in that kind of relationship? He lived in our house with my mom and my brother, so it wasn't like we were on our own. And I could always talk to Mom if there were any problems. She was more connected and aware of what was going on than most mothers. She knew I was at that age where I was going to be looking around. Either it was going to be in weird situations or it was going to be in my house, in my room.'

Angelina has always been very insistent that it was her mother, not her father, who instilled in her a love of acting, given that it was her mum who would take the kids on regular trips to the theatre and cinema. One thing her mum didn't anticipate, however, was that these outings would spark her daughter's fascination with knives. 'I went to the Renaissance Fair when I was a little girl and there were all these knives. There's something really beautiful and traditional about them. Different countries have different weapons and blades and there's something beautiful about them to me. So I began collecting knives. I've collected weapons since I was a little girl.'

The seed was planted. And her relationship with the punk-rock boyfriend would allow Angelina to push boundaries with the knives that she found so fascinating. She has said of this time, 'Some people go shopping – I cut myself. I started having sex and sex didn't feel like enough and my emotions didn't feel like enough. My emotions kept wanting to break out. In a moment of wanting something honest, I grabbed a knife and cut my boyfriend – and he cut me. He was a really good person, a sweet guy – not threatening, not scary. We had this exchange of something and we were covered in blood and my heart was racing and it was something dangerous. Life suddenly felt more honest than whatever this "sex" was supposed to be. It felt so primitive and it felt so honest, but then I had to deal with not telling my mother, hiding things, wearing gauze bandages to school.'

She has also said, 'It was a desperate need to feel. When I was young, I didn't have a "self" of my own. As I grew up, I lived through the characters I played, and became lost in different parts of my personality.' During one S&M session, Jolie asked her lover to draw a blade across her jawline and there is still a faint scar there today. 'Looking back,' says

Jolie, 'he was somebody that I wanted to help me break out and I would get frustrated when he couldn't help me.'

The cutting couldn't help her either – in fact, it nearly killed her. After one particular incident where Jolie slashed her neck, cut an X into her arm and sliced into her stomach, she was rushed to hospital. 'I nearly cut my jugular vein,' she admitted in 2000. 'By the time I was 16, I had gotten it [self-harming] all out of my system.'

Perhaps it was the getting it out of her system, or the near-death experience, that spelled the end of her relationship with the punk. Whatever the motivation, Angelina clearly felt it was time to move on. 'When she was 16, Angie decided that she'd had it with living with her mum and her boyfriend,' says Jean. 'She took an apartment across the street and moved. The boyfriend assumed he was moving in with her, but she kicked him out and that was the end of the relationship.'

Angelina herself has described it as a 'tough break-up. That relationship felt like a marriage. He cried a lot and it was just a load of high drama that I could do without.'

Whether Bertrand was glad to be rid of her unruly daughter is not known, but the neighbours certainly were. One of them remembers an occasion when the police had to be called because of the loud music coming from the flat in the early hours of the morning: 'My God, they would wake the dead, dancing and yelling and playing their music. It was a happy day when she moved.'

19

With hindsight, Jolie is aware of how self-indulgent she was in her teens, worrying about issues that, in the grand scale of things, don't really matter. Referring to these years, the actress has said, 'The doctor was probably going on about my father and mother while I was doing acid and bleeding under my clothes. I think now that, if someone would have taken me at 14 and dropped me in the middle of Asia or Africa, I'd have realised how self-centred I was, and that there was real pain and real death and real things to fight for. I wouldn't have been fighting myself so much.'

chapter 2

drama queen

Despite her early aspirations to be a funeral director, it was clear from the time she was a toddler, and putting on shows for her brother, that acting was in Angelina Jolie's blood. Not that she would admit it. In an interview with *People Weekly* in 2004, Jolie recalled, 'Growing up, I couldn't have cared less about movies. He [James, her brother] used to drag me to them. Jamie always loved film. He should've been the one who was working first.'

In the same interview, however, James begged to differ, insisting that it was his little sister who was the more theatrical of the two, particularly when he pointed a camera in her face. 'I'd tell her to act for me. We did a version of a Subway commercial, of her saying something like, "I'll punch your face if you don't buy a sandwich."'

Theses were fairly strong words for such a young girl, but

Angelina would be the first to admit that she was much tougher than her brother. 'We're almost perfect opposites. He never swears. I swear like a truck driver when I'm angry. When it comes to the moral high ground, he wins. When it comes to being loud and crass and tough, that's me.'

Jolie's parents readily encouraged her acting aspirations. 'I remember Jamie pointing the home video camera at me and saying "Come on, Angie, give us a show!" Neither [Dad] nor Mom ever said, "Be quiet! Stop talking!" I remember [Dad] looking me in the eye and asking, "What are you thinking? What are you feeling?"' Never one to be straightforward, Jolie has explained her theatrical interest in cryptic terms: 'I didn't know exactly what I wanted, but I knew I could know. I loved some kind of expression. I want[ed] so much to try to explain things to somebody… I'm very good at trying to explore different emotions and listen to people and feel things. That is an actor, I think.'

She might not have known what she wanted, but according to her dad it was inevitable she would end up in front of a camera. 'Looking back, there was evidence at an early that she would be an actor,' he said. 'She would take anything and make an event out of it. She was always very busy and creative and dramatic.'

When Marcheline moved her family back to LA, it seemed like the natural thing for 11-year-old Angelina to enrol in the Lee Strasberg Theatre Institute – given that her mother had once studied there. Lee Strasberg was an actor, director, producer and acting coach who had started up his LA drama school in 1969. Among the Hollywood greats who benefited from his teaching were James Dean, Robert De Niro, Steve McQueen, Jane Fonda, Al Pacino and Paul Newman. Marilyn Monroe was another: the pair were so close that in her final will she left Strasberg total control of 75 per cent of her estate and, as his favourite student, she actually moved in with him and his family at one point. Strasberg was a big advocate of method acting (the practice of actors drawing on their own memories, experiences and emotions to create a realistic performance) and it was perhaps for this very reason that Angelina quit the school after two years and several appearances in stage productions, claiming that she 'didn't have enough memories' to portray characters in the way she should. Strasberg's theories clearly stayed with her, though – Jolie would later say of her craft, 'Acting is not pretending or lying. It's finding a side of yourself that's the character and ignoring your other sides. And there's a side of me that wonders what's wrong with being completely honest.'

Having left the Strasberg Institute, Angelina went on to attend Beverly Hills High, from where she graduated at the age of 16. This was at the same time that she ditched the aforementioned punk-rocker boyfriend and moved into an apartment of her own. It was also around this time that she would start to seek help a bit closer to home and take acting lessons from her award-winning father. According to Voight, 'She'd come over to my house and we'd run through a play together, performing various parts. I saw that she had real talent. She loved acting. So I did my best to encourage her, to coach her and to share my best advice with her. For a while we were doing a new play together every Sunday.' Voight never claimed a stake in his daughter's eventual success, though. 'I gave her what help I could in terms of acting, but she went out and made a career of her own. It was all her doing and now I do my part by being as supportive as I can and giving advice when she asks for it.'

While most actors actively discourage their children from entering the world of showbiz, Voight was unperturbed by the challenges the film industry can throw at young people. In an interview in 2003, he said, 'People sometimes ask me if I'm glad my children got into this business. But I think, if young people have some kind of thing within themselves, a purpose, a dream or a vocation, then it should be acknowledged and encouraged. I always wanted to find out what my children wanted to do and then support them. I don't think we've ever been worried, because every life has its pitfalls.'

He and Marcheline must have had an inkling that their children would have the stars in their sights when they named them: the reason Angelina and James were given such exotic middle names (Jolie and Haven, respectively) was so that if they ever wanted to act they would have a stage name at the ready. He was also keen to encourage his daughter's imagination: when she was growing up, he let her believe that she was part Iroquois, from her mother's side, in an attempt to enhance his ex-wife's exotic background. 'We always liked the idea of her as an Iroquois and I love that my kids have picked up on that.' Even into adulthood, Angelina claimed that she had Iroquois blood, and at one point even campaigned for the tribe to allow her to join them in their 'sweat lodge'!

Of her dad's opinion regarding her desire to become an actress, Angelina has said, 'When I decided to become an actress, he didn't force me; he knew I wanted to do it on my own. I dropped my name [Voight] because it was important that I was my own person. But now it's great because we can talk on a level few people can talk to their parents on. Not only can we talk about our work, but our work is about our emotions, our lives, the games we play, what goes through our heads.'

Jolie found that by the age of 16 she had grown out of her awkward looks and was finally able to make a living out of modelling. She signed up with an agency called Finesse Model Management and modelled in both America and Europe, working mainly in New York, Los Angeles and London. She also made money appearing on screen in various music videos, including those by Meat Loaf ('Rock 'n' Roll Dreams Come Through'), The Rolling Stones ('Anybody Seen My Baby'), Lenny Kravitz ('Stand By My Woman'), Korn ('Did My Time') and The Lemonheads ('It's About Time'). Still very close to her brother James, she was more than happy to help him out with his student films for the USC School of Cinema, and appeared in five of the films he directed. She also went back to the Lee Strasberg school after graduating from high school and this is where she would land the first theatrical role that would get people talking.

When Angelina went along to audition for a part in *Room Service*, a comedy by John Murray and Allen Boretz, she decided that, rather than being conventional and going for a female role, she would challenge herself and land the part of a male dominatrix: 'I thought, you know, which character do I want to audition for? The big, fat, 40-year-old German man – that's the part for me.'

Voight was more than a little surprised when he went along to see his daughter's production. 'I was a little shocked seeing [Angelina] walk around as Frau Wagner. But the shock came from the realisation that, "Oh my God, she's just like me." She'll take these crazy parts and be thrilled that she can make people chuckle or whatever.'

Now financially independent, Angelina relocated to New York and enrolled in night classes (majoring in film) at New York University, but, by the age of 18, she had quit modelling 'because I couldn't take the pressure of always trying to be taller and skinnier and stuff' and landed her second film role. And unlike *Lookin' to Get Out*, securing the part had nothing to do with nepotism. In fact, it was around this time that Jolie had the Voight dropped from her name, believing that it was 'important to be her own person'.

Cyborg 2: Glass Shadow was a sequel to *Cyborg*, the 1989 original that had been a surprise hit at the box office. The original had launched the career of Jean Claude van Damme – or the 'Muscles from Brussels', as he later became known. Although he was fairly unknown at the time of the film's release, the beefy actor may have had something to do with the film's success; he didn't appear in the sequel and the film didn't even make it into cinemas, going straight to video. It was set in 2074 and Jolie played a cyborg (a person who is aided by a mechanical or electronic device) – Casella Reese, aka Cash – who has been designed specifically to seduce her way into a rival manufacturer's headquarters and then self-detonate. Things don't exactly go to plan, though: Jolie's character falls in love with a human being, Colson Ricks, and the couple soon escape their predicament with the help of a cyborg mercenary.

As artistic vehicles go, this wasn't the best choice for the ambitious Angelina to showcase her acting talents, and unfortunately the most memorable thing about the film is the fact that she bared her breasts in it. The film's failure left the young actress feeling disillusioned with her craft and catapulted her into a depression so severe that at one point she even considered taking her own life. 'I didn't know if I wanted to live because I didn't know what I was living for,' she recalled in an interview in 2001. Jolie admits that she was unhappy in New York and felt very alone. 'I didn't have any close friends any more and the city just seemed cold and sad and strange… everything that was kind of romantic about New York just got very cold for me,' she said.

Jolie's thoughts turned to suicide once more and she even sat down one evening in a New York hotel room and wrote a note to the maid, telling her to contact the police so that she didn't have to discover the body. At the last minute, however, Jolie found that she couldn't go through with it. 'I didn't know if I could pull the final thing across my wrists,' she admitted.

Wandering the streets of New York, she spotted a beautiful kimono that she wanted to buy, and suddenly realised that, by killing herself, she'd never actually be able to wear it. It was when she got back to her hotel room that she realised she couldn't go through with her desperate plan. 'I kind of lay there with myself and thought, "You might as well live a lot, really hard and not give a shit, because you can always walk through that door." So I started to live as if I could die any day.'

Perhaps it was this 'seize the day' attitude that led Angelina to her second significant film role – and, in turn, her second significant relationship.

chapter 3

here's jonny

'When I was 14, I visited London for the first time,' revealed Jolie a few years ago. 'And that's when I discovered my problem. English men appear to be so reserved, but underneath they're expressive, perverse and wild. All the insane moments in my life have happened with English men.'

With this in mind, it was perhaps inevitable that, at the age of 19, Angelina would fall for British actor Jonny Lee Miller on the set of *Hackers*. Directed by Iain Softley, this film follows a group of young people who are trying to prevent the unleashing of a dangerous computer virus while being pursued by the US Secret Service. Miller and Jolie play computer-literate teens (Dade Murphy and Kate Libby respectively) who get caught up in the corporate scam after accidentally hacking into the computer system of a huge conglomerate. It was Miller's first film (he would go on to land the role of Sickboy in *Trainspotting*, his most famous role to date, a year later) and Jolie's first experience of a major studio picture.

Film critics were fairly underwhelmed by *Hackers* and it was something of a flop, but Angelina knew that, as a woman, she couldn't afford to turn parts down so early on in her career. 'Dad sticks to this philosophy that any film he does should always say something positive or he won't do them,' she said. 'I want to be the same, but I've got to be realistic. There was less quantity and more quality when he started. I've got to be less picky. It's hard being a young actress now; no one wants you to keep your clothes on.'

If anything, Jolie was quite relieved that *Hackers* wasn't a huge success, because it meant she was less likely to be typecast in the future. 'I was a bit scared that, if the movie went really big, it would be something to remembered by. Don't get me wrong, I loved working with Iain, but I don't want to be stuck in that character forever.'

If anything, *Hackers* is only remembered for the fact that it introduced Jolie to her first husband, because, as Dade and Kate fell in love on screen, so too did Jonny and Angelina.

As soon as they laid eyes on each other, the attraction between the co-stars was evident. And Jolie, who had been celibate since she'd split up with her punk boyfriend three years previously, was more than ready to let a new man into her life. She said of meeting Jonny, 'We met while filming

Hackers and I always fall in love while I'm working on a film. It's such an intense thing, being absorbed into the world of a movie. It's like discovering you have a fatal illness, with only a short time to live. So you live and love twice as deep.'

Little did Jolie know how relevant this statement would become in terms of her future relationships.

The young cast of *Hackers* spent many weeks together preparing for the film, learning about computers (although Miller admitted that, out of ten, he'd give himself 'about a quarter' in terms of computer literacy, even by the end of filming) and it was this quality time that allowed the two young leads to fall in love.

'We had three weeks of learning how to type and rollerblade,' says Jolie, 'and hanging out with the cast, which was heaven – racing Jonny on rollerblades was a big part of our relationship. We read a lot about computers and met computer hackers. With a lot of lines, I didn't know what I was talking about, but it was fascinating.'

Born in middle-class Kingston-upon-Thames, Surrey, in 1972, Jonny found filming in New York (the location for the movie) something of an eye opener. He described the experience as 'brilliant. Filming at three in the morning under Brooklyn Bridge – it's stuff that you don't get to do if you're from Kingston.' He also joked that it wasn't much of a stretch playing Angelina's love interest saying, 'Yeah, it was terrible. You really have to suspend your disbelief!'

Much as it had been with Angelina, acting was in Jonny's blood and by the age of seven he knew he wanted his future to be in films. His great-grandfather, Edmund James Lee, was a music-hall performer; his grandfather, Bernard Lee, played M in the first dozen Bond films; and his father, Alan Miller, was a stage actor and, later, a stage manager, so the young Jonny certainly had plenty of people to go to for acting tips. While he was at Tiffin School for Boys, Miller attended drama classes at the National Youth Music Theatre and, as soon as he'd completed his GCSEs, at the age of 17, he left school to pursue a stage career.

Miller was 22 when he landed the role in *Hackers* and he'd never met anyone quite like Angelina before. He was bowled over by both her beauty and her talent: 'She's smart. She's resisted the usual stuff that a beautiful young actress would get... I think she'll rocket. I bloody hope so – she deserves it.'

Although the two actors were quite opposite in nature – she was outspoken and bolshy, he was shy and introverted – the seed of love had been sown and the couple eloped to Los Angeles in March 1996, six months after *Hackers* was released. This isn't to say that Jonny had an easy time seducing Angelina. He has since admitted that he 'chased [Angelina] all over the world. I chased her all over North America until she succumbed. It took a while – a good few thousand miles.'

He also had to deal with the fact that, after falling in love with her on the set of *Hackers*, Angelina told him that caring about someone so deeply made her sad and that after filming was finished he should forget about her. This was easier said than done, though, and an unperturbed Jonny continued to keep in touch in spite of her trying to push him away.

Next, Jolie went on to make *Mojave Moon*, a road movie. She played a girl named Ellie who hitches a ride from an older man, Al McCord (played by Danny Aiello), back to where her mother Julie (Anne Archer) lives in the Mojave Desert. Jolie put in a good performance as the lovestruck Ellie, who falls for Al over the course of the road trip, but the film was – again – instantly forgettable and didn't exactly set the world on fire. She made two more fairly low-key films, before going on to make *Foxfire*, on which she would yet again fall for one of her co-stars. In the thriller *Without Evidence*, she plays a junkie, Jodie Swearingen, and in *Love is All There is* she takes on the role of the romantic lead, Gina Malacici, in a modern-day version of *Romeo and Juliet*. In terms of impact, at least on a personal level, *Foxfire* was the next most significant film Jolie made. Although she and Jonny continued to speak to each other, they weren't 'committed' in the relationship sense, which was probably just as well given that Jolie went on to fall in love with someone else. And this time, it was a woman.

Foxfire told the tale of five teenage girls who formed an unlikely bond after beating up a teacher who had sexually harassed them. In the same way that she bonded with Jonny on the set of *Hackers*, Angelina became very close to Jenny Shimizu, the Japanese-American model turned actress who is most famous for appearing in the Calvin Klein CK One adverts. Angelina said of meeting Jenny, 'I fell in love with her the first second I saw her. I wanted to kiss and touch her. I noticed her sweater and the way her pants fitted and I thought, "My God!" I was getting incredibly strong sexual feelings. I realised I was looking at her in a way I look at men. It never crossed my mind that one day I was going to experiment with a woman. I just happened to fall for a girl.'

Jenny was similarly taken with Angelina and described their courtship as being more emotional than sexual in the early stages. 'During breaks in filming *Foxfire*, I got to sit down with this person [Angelina] and spend two weeks with them, meeting them and talking with them before anything got sexual. I actually felt like I was caring for someone more than simply just having sex. And I didn't feel like there was a straight girl that I was just bedding and she was going to freak out the next morning. We had established such a nice relationship that I felt this girl would have me back, no matter what. I knew this person would be loyal and wonderful to me.'

The girls didn't just hang out on set, but spent a lot of time together after filming was finished. 'We used to visit strip clubs,' says Jenny, 'and there was this tension. After the second week of filming, we kissed. She is beautiful.

Her mouth is amazing. I've never kissed anyone with a bigger mouth than Angelina. It's like two water beds – it's like this big kind of warm, mushy, beautiful thing. She's a gorgeous woman.'

The only fly in Jenny and Angelina's ointment was the presence of Jonny in Jolie's life, and, although men often fantasise about lesbian sex, the reality was that Angelina's new relationship didn't turn him on one bit. Jenny said of the love triangle, 'We were already sleeping together when I met Jonny while on *Foxfire*. She told both of us how she felt and we all went out to dinner one night. She was honest – that's how she's been her whole life.'

As an openly sexual person and someone who isn't scared to push boundaries, it wouldn't be a surprise if Angelina had suggested her two lovers get together and indulged in a threesome, but according to Jenny this was never on the cards. 'We didn't have a threesome,' she said. 'I'm not really into that – it was a friendship the three of us had. But there wasn't much conversation with Jonny. I think he was very threatened by me.'

And who can blame him? The man was desperately in love and, having chased her halfway round the world, he wanted some commitment from Jolie – not to hear that she was in love with a woman. Jenny's gut instinct was right and Jonny has since admitted that jealousy in a relationship is one of his least desirable traits. 'I've learned that jealousy is to be avoided at all costs. I'm a really horribly jealous person, but I've calmed down now,' he said after his divorce from Jolie.

By this time, Angelina had established quite a reputation as an S&M queen and Jenny didn't escape Jolie's fascination with knives. 'It's not so much we were dressed in leather capes and masks and there were chains. It was emotional. I would restrain her with my arms but we didn't get into buying stuff. We just used whatever props were available if we wanted to. She was a collector of knives and taught me about them.' Jenny also described Angelina as 'a very dominant personality. Once she displays love for you, she wants to know how much you care about her.'

Although Jolie says that her attraction to Jenny took her by surprise, prior to meeting Jenny she had admitted that her modelling days had helped her to see women in a sexual light. 'I did some modelling years ago and shared a cabin with one woman. I was in my black pants and T-shirt, watching television. She was in a little g-string putting lotion on her whole body, with nail care too, making sure every single inch of her legs were shaved. It was sexy for me to see a woman like that. She looked all glossy and I wanted to eat her. You have to live for moments like that.'

Despite these homosexual inclinations, Angelina maintained that her desires did not necessarily change her sexual orientation. 'I don't want to be provocative and say I'm bisexual, but I understand the love of one woman [for] another because I've felt it. I believe you love people whether they're a man or a woman. I like everything. Boyish girls, girlish boys, the heavy and the skinny. Which is a problem when I'm walking down the street.'

We can only assume that it was a problem for Jonny too, but his chasing Angelina paid off in the end: Jolie finally expressed the commitment he had long been seeking, and married him. Miller described their wedding day as 'very romantic', while Jolie has said of the nuptials, 'We didn't have a big white wedding, we had a small black wedding.'

As showbiz weddings go, it was definitely one of the more 'out there' ceremonies, with Angelina wearing black leather trousers and a white shirt with her husband's name scrawled on the back in her own blood. 'I consider it poetic,' she said after the wedding. 'Some people write poetry, others give themselves a little cut. It meant a lot.'

Although Jonny had admitted that he was 'involved with an American girl who lived in LA' and Angelina was open about the fact that they'd shared an apartment throughout the *Hackers* shoot, the couple had tried to keep their relationship under wraps initially. This all changed after the wedding, however, and, in her typically candid style, Angelina would be completely open in interviews about her life with Jonny. Of their hasty marriage, she said, 'The way we both feel about life is to live in the moment and not think of the future. Even if we divorce, I would have been married to somebody I really loved and know what it was to be a wife for a few years. Marriage is no

37

bigger deal than signing a piece of paper that commits you to someone forever.'

From this statement alone, we can detect that, for Angelina, the marriage may have been more of an experiment than a lifelong commitment, and ultimately it was her lack of commitment that would drive the union into an early grave. She had rather flippantly commented that she 'would have married Jenny if I hadn't married Jonny' and Shimizu said of her lover, 'I don't think there's any way of controlling Angelina. She goes looking for excitement all the time. I can't imagine her just being married and being happy.'

Miller was a bit more optimistic about the marriage, saying simply, 'When you love somebody, you want to be with them. We are a couple who are into extremes and the extreme is to get married. Having this eye-opening and honest relationship really opens doors within yourself.'

Perhaps one of the metaphorical 'doors' Jonny was referring to was the fact that he and his wife enjoyed a very experimental sexual relationship. Equally unconventionally, the couple even had a pet albino corn snake living in a tank at the end of their bed. 'It was kept in a glass cage in the bedroom,' said Jonny. 'We had to find it another home in the end because we couldn't give it the love and attention it deserved. You've got to give a snake a lot of love, or they turn into right bitches.' He also revealed that they fed the snake mice that he had killed for it, saying, 'I won't tell you how I did it, because I will have all sorts of people leaving bombs on my doorstep, but I will say I'm very, very quick.'

While many men might have been intimidated by Jolie's S&M tendencies and affection for pet snakes, Miller was clearly more than a match for the actress. She once described him as 'pretty wild' and on another occasion commented, 'The English might be repressed but they're good in bed!' There aren't many Hollywood actresses who would openly discuss their sex lives, but, as part of her quest to be as honest with her fans as she possibly could be, the young Angelina willingly went into detail about how she liked things to be in the bedroom. 'I have always felt really naughty. I got involved in an S&M lifestyle and there were some people a lot further down that road than me. I had to be careful because I am an actress and recognisable. It fascinates me, though. I always felt that, if someone approached me to try something, then I would be the last person to walk away. I'd have a go.'

She also talked about her fascination with domination. 'I used to think dominating was the thing to do. But then I realised that the person who was dominating was really the slave, because they did all the hard work. They are exhausted, while the other person was lying there enjoying it. I thought, "I'm not getting anything for me." So I changed to thinking on the lines of being both master and slave.'

Whether Jonny was her 'master' or her 'slave', it's clear that he was willing to experiment, and, while promoting *Dracula* (in which he starred) in 2001, he admitted that he had sucked his ex-wife's blood and that, 'She digs that kind of thing.' And he certainly enjoyed the reputation she gave him for being wild in the sack, admitting after the marriage was over that her S&M anecdotes were 'good for my image'.

Jolie was Miller's first long-term serious relationship, and there's no doubt that he was madly in love, but even he was aware of the relationship's downfalls. 'It's been up, down and crazy. It does help her being an actress. You understand each other and the need to have your space.'

For a while, things were good between the two, with Jonny moving into Angelina's LA apartment as soon as they were married. This was a big change in environment for the Surrey boy, but he explained that it was a professional decision as much as it was a personal one. 'Being nuts about her had something to do with it [the move] but I also had to think it was a great opportunity to explore other worlds and to move and to work in Los Angeles with a purpose. Otherwise I might have been thinking "what if" for the rest of my life.'

Due to the whirlwind nature of their relationship, Miller didn't actually meet Angelina's father until after the wedding and was understandably nervous about his first meeting with Jon Voight. 'It was a pretty weird experience, saying, "Hello, I'm your son-in-law" to Jon Voight. But Jon's a nice man and we all breathe the same air.' Of his own parents' reaction to the bizarre nature of his wedding, Jonny has said, 'Well, they do actually have a photo album of the wedding. It wasn't as gruesome as it sounds. I think [people] imagine some kind of satanic ceremony. It wasn't like that.'

Unfortunately, it was the aforementioned need for 'space' that would hinder the relationship in the end, with Angelina admitting that she wasn't able to give her husband the time and attention he deserved. 'It's just that I wasn't being a wife. I think we really needed to grow and we always talked about getting remarried. But he really had to put up with quite a lot. Certainly, my career is first. And, for some reason, I seem to meet a lot of men who say they are like that but, for some reason, it just doesn't turn out that way.'

We can deduce from this that Jonny was willing to put his relationship before his career, but the same could not be said of his wife. And Angelina would be the first to admit that her strong desire for independence could well have been a direct result of her parents' divorce. 'I don't know if my childhood was any worse than anyone else's, but it is disturbing and sad when you see one parent figure not respecting the other. That probably had a great effect on me wanting to be self-sufficient. I was raised feeling that I didn't want the ground to be taken away from me, and so, by the age of 14, I was already working [as a model]. I didn't want to ask for help from anybody, and that extended into my own marriages.'

As much as she loved Jonny, Angelina was unable to give herself up entirely – unfortunately for him, he met her at a time when her career was of the utmost importance to her.

'I'm not present enough, physically or emotionally, in relationships to get serious. It's not fair to the other person that I'm so busy with my career and that I'm often distant even when I am with someone.'

For a while, the couple continued to live together, but emotionally they were miles apart. Angelina said, 'We were living side by side, but we had separate lives. I wanted more for him than I could give. He deserves more than I am prepared to give at this time in my life, but there is a very good possibility that we could get married again some time in the future.'

In the end, the couple's fate was sealed when, after tiring of LA, Angelina wanted to relocate to New York. By this time, Jonny was homesick and, if he was going to move anywhere, it would be back to London; he described New York as 'too claustrophobic'. 'I know this sounds mad, but I was missing little things like the Nine O'Clock News, red buses, country smells, the sound of our rock music, *Match of the Day*. Angie wanted to move to New York instead. I didn't want to experience a whole new town again, so I came back and moved into a flat in London.'

Initially, the couple visited each other, but Jolie admitted that the distance had caused an even larger gulf between them, and she came to feel that visiting his abode in London just didn't seem right. 'It's not my house, though he wants me to feel right at home. It doesn't feel right for me to walk in on him in the shower, or for me to wander about naked.'

The couple made the inevitable decision to split, but remarkably they only had good things to say about each other in the aftermath, with Jolie describing their marriage as 'a great experience', saying that it had 'enriched both our lives' but that she 'knew it wouldn't last forever'. She also said that, despite their problems, the relationship hadn't been a destructive one. 'Jonny and I never fought and we never hurt each other. I really wanted to be his wife. I really wanted to commit.'

Although he didn't resent his ex-wife (or, if he did, he certainly never spoke publicly about it), it is clear that Miller was the more heartbroken of the two. He said in an interview afterwards, 'I think love exists. You don't know for how long, though. It rarely lasts forever.' After the divorce, Jonny was asked if he still believed in love at first sight, to which he replied, 'Yeee-ah. Well, I believe in something at first sight. Love is based on trust, though. You can't know that on sight.' The actor was understandably reluctant to attract attention to his feelings, and, when asked if anyone had ever broken his heart, he admitted, 'Yeah, they have, but I can't tell you that. Because you'll know who it was.' He also admitted that marriage was something he 'wouldn't rush to do again'.

As ill-suited as they were as husband and wife, it's clear that there was a lot of love between these two and, despite getting hurt, Miller definitely didn't see the marriage as a mistake. 'There are no regrets. Marriage was something that didn't work out, and I had to make a decision sooner or later. I decided to make it sooner. We still have a really good relationship. In fact, we've found that our new relationship suits us both… One of the main reasons it broke up was that I got fed up of Hollywood. I enjoyed it at first, but realised that Britain is the place to be, both for work and personal contentment. We're extremely good friends. I speak to her all the time. It's not black and white.'

And to all the critics who said the union wouldn't last from the start, Miller had this to say: 'People find it bizarre and extraordinary that we were together. To me, it's not. Angelina's image is of a wild, crazy femme fatale. She's not. She's a very nice, very generous person. A big-hearted girl. She just says what's she's feeling. She doesn't get up to any more mischief than your average person… well, maybe a little bit.'

And so, with Angelina in New York and Jonny back in London, the marriage was officially over. No one regretted the end of the relationship more than Jolie, who would admit years later, 'Divorcing Jonny was probably the dumbest thing I've ever done, but I don't dwell on it. I was so lucky to have met the most amazing man, who I wanted to marry. It comes down to timing. I think he's the greatest husband a girl could ask for. I'll always love him, we were simply too young.'

chapter 4

winning over the critics

After *Foxfire*, Jolie felt utterly disillusioned with the acting world and seriously contemplated giving it up. None of her films had been huge commercial successes and, as yet, she had gone largely unnoticed by critics, although many had noted that the young actress had potential. All this changed, however, when she landed a role in two TV films, which would finally get her the recognition she both craved and deserved.

The first was *George Wallace*, which starred Gary Sinise as the infamous Alabama governor. Jolie played Wallace's second wife Cornelia and her superb performance went on to earn her a Golden Globe for Best Supporting Actress in a Series, Mini Series or Motion Picture Made For Television. Jolie thanked the director George Frankenheimer for being 'brilliant' and later gave him the biggest compliment of all by crediting him and the film's production crew with reinstating her faith in acting. '*Wallace* was the first thing I did where I felt their ideas were better than mine,' she said. In a speech similar to the one she would make years later when she won an Oscar for *Girl, Interrupted*, her family also came out well. Jolie gushed, 'Mom, stop crying, stop screaming. It's OK, Jamie, my brother, my best friend, I couldn't do anything without you. I love you so much. Dad, where are you? Hi. I love you. Thank you so much. Thank you.'

The second TV part that would secure Jolie's place on the Hollywood map was the lead role in *Gia*, the HBO biopic about the life of the drug-abusing supermodel Gia Marie Carangi. Born on 29 January 1960, Carangi was a supermodel in the late 1970s and early 1980s and her life story is one of great success and, ultimately, great tragedy. Plucked from obscurity from her hometown of Philadelphia at the tender age of 18, Carangi's meteoric rise in the fashion world proved to be too much for the young model to cope with and, soon after settling into the party lifestyle of New York's fashion set, she became addicted to cocaine. Carangi, who was of Italian, Welsh and Irish ancestry, was a photographer's dream, given that the success of Janice Dickinson had stemmed a desire for exotic-looking models. Dickinson and Carangi were regulars at the New York's legendary Studio 54 disco, and Dickinson later said of this time, 'We loved it. It was a place for us. A place where we could be with the beautiful, do drugs, be out of our minds and it all seemed normal.'

Unfortunately, Gia's drug taking went far beyond the point of being 'normal' and, by 1980, she was turning up at photo shoots in a terrible state; she'd sneak off to inject heroin, have violent temper tantrums and sometimes even fall asleep in front of the camera. By 1981, she'd fallen out of favour in the fashion world and entered rehab. Gia's most prominent relationships were with women and, by the time she was trying to wean herself off drugs, she had fallen in love with a student named Elyssa Stewart (who went by the name of Rochelle). Gia's recovery was not helped by the fact that Rochelle also had a drug problem and Carangi fell off the wagon when Chris von Wangenheim, a fashion photographer who she'd been very close to, died in a car crash.

Carangi would shoot her last cover (for *Cosmopolitan*) in 1982 with her hands behind her back so as to conceal the scars left on her arms left by heroin injection, but her glory days were over and her good friend Francesco Scavullo, the photographer who worked with her on the shoot, said that the 'wonderful spirit she had was gone'. By 1983, Gia had started working as a prostitute (she was raped on several occasions) and by 1984 she was diagnosed with AIDS, then a newly recognised disease. The disease eventually claimed Gia's life and she died at the age of 26 on 18 November 1986. Although no one from the fashion world attended the funeral in Philadelphia (her mother had her transferred to

Philadelphia's Hanhemann University Hospital in the final months of her life), everyone she had worked with mourned the loss of the beautiful girl who had once had the fashion world at her feet.

The role of Gia would become all consuming for Angelina – who was never one to do anything by halves. At first, she was hesitant about playing such a troubled and complex woman (indeed, she turned the role down four times) but once she'd accepted there was no going back, and her dedication to the production would even have a detrimental effect on her marriage. Jolie said, 'Gia has enough similarities to me that I figured this would either be a purge of all my demons or it was really going to mess with me.'

Jolie and Miller's relationship – already on the rocks – was not helped by her immersion in the life of the supermodel, and when she was filming she would not even communicate with her husband. (At one point, she told him, 'I'm alone; I'm dying; I'm gay; I'm not going to see you for weeks.') Although there can be no doubt that Miller admired his wife's dedication to her craft, it was clear to him that he was not the most important thing in her life, which Jolie herself admits was one of the main reasons for the breakdown of their relationship. In fact, for the duration of filming, Jolie cut herself off from everyone, choosing 'not to do anything, not to have friends, not hang out'.

Although playing Gia was by far her most challenging role to date, Jolie and Carangi had a lot in common and there can be no doubt that the actress drew on a lot of her own experiences when it came to portraying the model. Both women felt like outsiders when they were growing up, both had experimented with their sexuality, both were models and suffered at the hands of the fickle industry and, most importantly, both women had let drugs come to play a part in their life. While Jolie's experimentation with drugs was nowhere near as serious or problematic as Gia's addiction, her experience must have helped her to understand this aspect of the model's character. That said, Jolie had little time for the character to whom she was dedicating so much of her energy. After seeing her doing an interview on a show called *20/20* in 1983, Jolie came to the conclusion that the model was false and unlikeable, saying, 'I hated her. She spoke with this affected accent and was acting her butt off.'

She may not have liked Carangi, but playing her was certainly helpful to Angelina in the sense that it showed her a path she didn't want to go down. 'I've definitely needed to learn the lessons Gia needed to learn. Especially feeling that the physical is more important than anything else, or that you're only as smart as good as somebody thinks you are. It's been really important for me to look at myself in the mirror and realise that I can't let myself go down like she did.' And she was the first to admit that she and the model shared some similarities. 'She was a lot like me, although the key to her was she needed to be loved. I want to be

49

understood. Maybe that's the same. She was a good person who self-destructed when things went bad.'

Playing Gia may have troubled the actress, but the film's director, Michael Cristofer, was certain he'd made the right choice in casting her and had nothing but praise for Jolie's attitude. 'She's a hunter,' he said. 'I think most of us are cowards; we live at home in our nice little worlds, and the artists are the ones who come along, the adventurers, who go out into the dark away from the campfire, and then they come back and tell us the story of their adventures. She's one of those people. Life is an adventure for her.'

Jolie had always been incredibly candid about her life, and has always maintained that her fans should know all her flaws and weaknesses so as to have a realistic view of her, and not assume that because she's in the public eye her life is perfect. Jolie says, 'Wouldn't it be more helpful for a young girl to know of the things I've discovered, the mistakes I've made, of how human I am, and how like her I am? That's more interesting than, "Here is how much stuff she has and how fabulous her life is."'

Jolie has a point, but there's one topic which the actress has always remained far more tight-lipped about – presumably through fear of being a negative role model – and that topic is heroin.

While she is fairly open about other drugs she has experimented with, Jolie has said very little about her use of heroin, although she has gone as far as to admit that she liked it and that at one point it 'meant a lot to her'. And, if Jonny Lee Miller did one thing for Jolie while they were together, it was to get her away from the life-threatening situations she had previously put herself in. Jolie says, 'I have done just about every drug possible. Cocaine, ecstasy, LSD and, my favourite, heroin. Although I have been through a lot of dark days, Jonny helped me see the light.' When pushed on the topic of her use of heroin, however, Jolie stated flatly, 'I don't want to go into detail.'

The actress is far more open about other drugs, such as cannabis, and recalls how, of all the drugs she took, it had the biggest effect on her. 'The worst effect, oddly enough, was pot, which made me feel out of control and I became silly and giggly. I liked LSD for a while until I went to Disneyland and started thinking about Mickey Mouse being a short middle-aged man in a costume who hates his life. My brain went the other way and I started thinking, "Look at all those fake flowers, the kids are on leashes, the parents hate being here." Those drugs can be dangerous. I know friends who are no longer happy or interesting, living for junk all the time and using people.'

Angelina's drug use certainly didn't make her dad happy, and Voight's brother Chip Taylor says that it was her teenage rebellion that ensured the father–daughter relationship's rocky path. 'She had some drug issues and Jon was real concerned about that, and then she did all this cutting herself, and the tattoos…'

Obviously Jon found most of his daughter's lifestyle decisions hard to understand and this is a theme that would continue in their relationship until the present day.

She may have put all personal relationships on hold for her part in *Gia*, but the hard work and sacrifices paid off and in 1999 Jolie won two awards for her portrayal of the tragic figure – a Golden Globe for Best Actress in a Mini-Series or TV Film and a Screen Actors Guild Award for Best Female Actor in a TV Movie or Mini-Series.

Ironically, considering the critical acclaim her performance would garner, Angelina felt disillusioned and exhausted by the end of *Gia* and had decided yet again to quit her profession for a while, saying, 'I felt like I'd given everything I had and I couldn't imagine what else was in me.'

Having spent months in the shoes of someone who was incredibly successful professionally but personally unfulfilled, Jolie was terrified that, if she carried on making films but having no home life to speak of, she'd end up like Gia. 'I was scared of getting public after that part, and seeing how undernourished her private life was, how malnourished she was, though her exterior was very glamorous,' admitted Jolie. 'So I'd be doing interviews and then going home by myself not knowing if I'd ever be in a relationship or good in marriage or a good mother or... complete as a woman.'

This feeling of apathy and lack of direction in her life caused Jolie to sink into another depression, which would again cause her to contemplate ending it all. But this time, Jolie had no intention of doing the deed herself and subsequently went to the dramatic lengths of actually hiring a hitman to kill her.

'This is going to sound insane, but there was a time I was going to hire somebody to kill me. The person spoke very sweetly to me, he made me think about it for a month. And, after a month, other things changed in my life and I was surviving again. With suicide comes all the guilt of people around you thinking they could have done something. With somebody being murdered, nobody takes some kind of guilty responsibility.'

Receiving the awards for *Gia* had again given Jolie the reassurance she needed and she finally felt like her contribution to the arts mattered. '*Gia* came out and people responded to it. Suddenly it seemed like people understood me. I thought my life was completely meaningless and that I would never be able to communicate anything and that there was nobody who understood… and then I realised that I wasn't alone. Somehow life changed.'

Her success in two major TV roles had given her the platform she required to further her film career. With her marriage to Jonny Lee Miller over and her depression behind her, Jolie was ready to move on, both professionally and personally.

Chapter 5

a work in progress

While Jolie's professional confidence was boosted by her warmly received TV roles, she had yet to become a big hitter on the Hollywood circuit, despite going out of her way to fight for roles that didn't just require her to look beautiful on screen. 'I'm having to do a lot just to keep my clothes on and not be cast in girlfriend roles,' she admitted in an interview she did with her father in June 1997.

Ironically, when Jolie made this statement she was in the middle of filming *Hell's Kitchen*, in which she played Gloria McNeary, the girlfriend of a robber, and had just finished filming *Playing God*, where she played Claire, the love interest of both Eugene Sands (David Duchovny) and Raymond Blossom (Timothy Hutton). *Playing God* follows a drug-addicted surgeon (Sands) who gets involved with a crime lord (Blossom) and falls in love with his girlfriend

(Claire) along the way. It was panned by critics, described by one as a 'miserable experience' and a 'piece of garbage'. Despite the onslaught of criticism, however, Jolie had a ball making the movie, describing the experience as 'very rock 'n' roll and fun and loud'.

Once again, Jolie found herself benefiting from the film on a more personal than professional level and, in the aftermath of her relationship with Jonny Lee Miller, she found herself falling for yet another one of her co-stars, this time in the shape of Timothy Hutton. Born in California in 1960, Hutton was 15 years Jolie's senior (when she was only five years old he won Best Supporting Actor for *Ordinary People*). Between the years of 1986 and 1990, Hutton was married to the actress Debra Winger and the marriage produced a son, Noah. Despite the substantial age gap, Jolie and Hutton had a great deal in common and, when they met, they felt like kindred spirits. Hutton also came from an acting background and, like Jolie, he had starred in a film – *Never Too Late* – with his dad Jim Hutton at the tender age of five. Timothy was also from a broken home and had moved around a lot as a child after his parents divorced when he was an infant.

Having come out of a relationship that suffered from a lack of maturity on both Jolie and Miller's part, the actress relished being in the company of an older man and loved Hutton so deeply that she had the letter H tattooed on the inside of her left wrist as a symbol of her affection. Angelina later stated that the H also represented her brother James Haven, which was fortunate considering her romance with Hutton would last no longer than a year. 'It was great while it lasted,' she said. 'He is a lovely sensitive guy and we could read each other very well, but in the end it just didn't work out.'

The H wasn't the first tattoo Angelina had had done. Since she had been a teenager, she had taken a great interest in body art. Unfortunately for her, it was yet another hobby of hers that was viewed with suspicion and only served to enhance her morbid reputation. 'People interpret things strangely,' she mused. 'I see tattoos as dark and romantic and tribal. And, anyway, I do feel as if all that stuff has been like some sly move on my part so that people will focus on the tattoos and knives and that way [they] won't really know anything about me. Yet everyone thinks they know personal stuff about me.' She also likes to think that her tattoos were an indication of her spontaneous nature. 'For me, they're all about the moment. Like when you jump out of a plane. I got one of my tattoos done in a tattoo parlour in Scotland by myself in the middle of the night. I don't regret it. It will always be a reminder of that moment.'

As well as the aforementioned H, Angelina had a Tennessee Williams quote on her left forearm ('A prayer for the wild at heart, kept in cages'), a Latin cross on the lower left of her abdomen, a large tiger on her back, a dragon under the tiger, 'Know your rights' under her neck between her shoulders, two pointy black tribals on her lower back,

57

'strength of will' written in Arabic on her right forearm and 'Quod me nutrit me destruit' (Latin for 'What nourishes me also destroys me') below her navel. She later went on to have 'Billy Bob' tattooed on her left arm as a tribute to her second husband as well as a tattoo on her right forearm with a secret meaning. After the two split, Jolie had the tattoos removed with the help of laser treatment and then had the co-ordinates representing the locations where her adopted children Maddox and Zahara hailed from tattooed on the place where 'Billy Bob' had been. One of the tattoos that Jolie has talked about most is a window she had done on her lower back, which represented the fact that she was always searching for something better in life. 'I had it done because at the time I was always looking out the window,' she said. 'I always wanted to be somewhere else. Now I don't. Now I'm happy.'

Jolie also marked Maddox's adoption with a large protection prayer on her left shoulder. The work was carried out by monks and was one of her particular favourites. 'There are five vertical rows of ancient Cambodian script, which are designed to ward off bad luck. I like it a lot. It looks very sacred.'

Although Angelina's tattoos proved to be a bit of a nightmare to cover up for make-up artists on film sets, she liked the fact that they often reduced the amount of nude scenes she'd be required to do, and felt that directors had to be more creative with sexy shots rather than just ordering her to take her clothes off. In terms of her career, a big concern of Jolie's had always been that she was hired on the basis of her looks and, by customising her own body, she felt like she regained some control and reduced the opportunities for her to shed her clothes.

In terms of the low-key films she made in the late nineties, *Playing By Heart* proved to be the most substantial for Jolie, if only because her performance as the LA clubber Joan won her the Best Breakthrough Performance By An Actress award from the National Board of Review. This romantic comedy follows the lives of 11 people living in LA who are all searching for love and, although the characters are seemingly unconnected, their stories converge by the end of the film. Jolie, who played the youngest female character opposite Ryan Phillippe (Keenan), was in good company in this ensemble drama and was joined by the likes of Patricia Clarkson, Sean Connery, Dennis Quaid and Gena Rowlands. As her award proves, Jolie more than held her own and the film was something of a sleeper hit.

With *The Bone Collector*, however, Jolie finally had a film role she could really sink her teeth into and focus on playing something other than the love interest. That said, this crime thriller does have a love story at the heart of it, but it is an unspoken and unconsummated love, which simmers slowly beneath the central plot. Here we see Jolie play a rookie cop, Amelia Donaghy, who reluctantly gets involved in solving a murder case with a quadriplegic homicide detective, Lincoln Rhyme (Denzel Washington). Confined to his bed and only able to move his head and one finger, Washington's character employs Amelia as his eyes and legs in order to solve the crime. Over the course of the film, the two characters develop a mutual professional respect for each other and subsequently enjoy a deep emotional connection. 'To me, they have the sexiest, most romantic love affair of any film I've ever done,' said Jolie. 'The disgusting truth is that you can have sex with anyone, but you can't have that connection where somebody can look into your eyes and see you and push you to be the best that you are. Though Denzel was a quadriplegic and we never touched, having him look into my eyes was more scary than having someone eat me.'

Jolie may have enjoyed the subtlety of the unspoken love between Lincoln and Amelia, but not everyone agreed with her. One unimpressed critic said, 'The only mystery in this movie worth solving is why it can show a woman being tortured and a man having his face devoured by rats but it can't show a black crippled cop kissing a white woman.'

Others also criticised the film for being 'formulaic, mindless and gory' and accused the plot of having 'more holes in it than a New York junkie'.

As harsh as the criticism was, very little was directed at Jolie and Washington, who were generally thought to have done the best they could with a weak script. And Jolie certainly did her best when it came to researching the role. Indeed, after visiting some real-life police officers to get a feel for their profession, she took home pictures of real corpses, in situ, so she would become accustomed to seeing such gruesome sights. We can only assume that this theory helped Jolie deal with some of the tougher scenes, but, given how depressed she had become after filming *Gia*, she would have known by then that sometimes she took her method acting a bit too far. 'I need to learn to relax and not prepare too much, just enjoy life,' she said. 'I notice that my characters go out to dinner and have fun and take these great trips, but I spend so much time on their lives, I don't have much of a personal life of my own. I have to sort of remember to fill out that little notebook on me.'

One person who applauded her dedication was the film's director, Phillip Noyce, who, like many other directors, had seen Angelina in *Gia* and felt that she was capable of anything. 'We were looking for a very specific actress for *The Bone Collector*,' he said. 'She had to be young, in her mid-twenties, with the strength to play a New York cop as well as a very special vulnerability. What I saw in Angelina's performance in *Gia* was all those qualities.'

With several big-name actresses begging for the role of Amelia, he really had to fight to get her on board, and was confronted with questions such as 'Angelina who?' from film bosses when he put her name forward. If *The Bone Collector* was considered a failure, it certainly wasn't down to Jolie's efforts – she had proved to everyone that she was capable of playing someone who wasn't just a pretty face. And, if we needed any more proof of Jolie's capabilities, she was to provide it in her next movie – which would turn out to be the most significant film in her entire career.

Chapter 6

girl, interrupted

When Susanna Kaysen wrote *Girl, Interrupted*, her memoirs describing the two years she spent in a mental hospital between the ages of 18 and 20, she could have had no idea that it would one day be made into an Oscar-winning film. Kaysen's book explores her experience of Boston's McLean Psychiatric Hospital (where she admitted herself after taking an overdose) in the late sixties. As someone who was no stranger to suicidal thoughts, Angelina read Susanna's account and fell in love with it instantly. For Jolie, one character in particular stood out, and she found herself highlighting all the sections that included Kaysen's fellow patient Lisa Rowe because she 'loved her and identified with her'. Jolie felt that the troubled and rebellious character, who was diagnosed as a sociopath, spoke to her and, when she heard that the book was being made into a film, she literally begged the producers for the part of Lisa.

Winona Ryder had been similarly affected by Kaysen's work when she read it at the age of 21 and, determined to have it made into a film, she tried to option the book – only to discover that Doug Wick, a producer, had got in there first. Ryder immediately contacted Doug but was dismayed to find that he'd been stopped in his tracks when Columbia Pictures told him they were unwilling to fund the film. Owing to the dark and challenging nature of the characters, they couldn't see its appeal and it wasn't until Ryder expressed a strong desire to play the lead role of Susanna that they changed their tune. They had a big star on board and big stars meant big audiences.

Like Jolie, Ryder, who was born in Minnesota in 1971, had herself suffered from psychological problems in the past and, after establishing her name in films such as *Heathers* (1989), *Mermaids* and *Edward Scissorhands* (both 1990), the actress checked herself into a hospital at the tender age of 20 to be treated for depression, anxiety attacks and exhaustion. Growing up in a commune in North Carolina, Winona – who was named after the town she was born in – hadn't had the most conventional of upbringings, and becoming very famous at such a young age had thrown up all sorts of insecurities and questions in her. In *Girl, Interrupted*, Kaysen explores the frustration of young women who feel misunderstood and Ryder felt that these sentiments should be given a platform. During her stay in hospital, Kaysen was diagnosed with borderline personality disorder, which is characterised by instability in mood, interpersonal relationships, self-image, identity and the individual sense of self. In the book, she questions her diagnosis and wonders whether she is really so different from many other girls her age who are struggling through adolescence.

Like Jolie, Ryder felt that it was important to be open about her own personal demons, so that young girls who had looked up to her since the cult hit *Heathers* realised that being rich, famous and successful didn't necessarily equate with personal happiness. 'Since I've talked about my anxiety, I've gotten a really good response. Young women were grateful to learn that it happens to everybody, even people they consider perfect.'

As soon as the film was given the go-ahead by Columbia, James Mangold (who went on to direct *Walk the Line* with Reese Witherspoon and Joaquin Phoenix) came on board as director and decided that he wanted to rewrite the script in order to make it 'a woman's picture with balls'. Knowing that he was the guy to talk to, Jolie contacted him and literally begged for the role of Lisa. As it turned out, there was no begging required, for, after seeing her audition, Mangold knew he had found the perfect person to portray the wild and outspoken Lisa, the character he had described as 'Jack Nicholson in drag'. He said of Jolie's audition, 'She sat down and she was Lisa. I felt like the luckiest guy on earth. Her power is volcanic, it's huge, it's electric.'

After Jolie's award-winning performances in *Gia* and *George Wallace*, Ryder, who was an executive producer on the film, was also keen to get her on board and knew that her screen presence was a force to be reckoned with. That said, the two actresses weren't exactly the best of friends on set, and given that Ryder saw this as her big chance to win an Academy Award it may well have hurt that it was Jolie who ended up stealing the show. As far as Jolie was concerned, their lack of closeness was mainly to do with the fact that Ryder spent all her free time with her then boyfriend Matt Damon, but, according to an insider on the set, Ryder would go to Jolie for comfort after filming harrowing scenes only to be told that she couldn't deal with her problems because it wasn't what Lisa would do. 'To play an anxiety attack,' said Ryder, 'you have to get an anxiety attack. And I didn't know how to put a lid on that.'

In response to Ryder's need for emotional support, Jolie would say, 'I need to not feel things. I need to not feel as if we are all together.' She herself described Lisa as 'a complete sociopath with no emotion and no sensitivity', so if nothing else you have to commend Jolie for her method acting!

According to Jolie, however, the film was a huge bonding experience and it was only her co-star that she didn't gel with. 'I was very social on this film, just not with Winona,' she said. 'That's just how it ended up.' As the matriarch of the ward, Lisa is one of the most dominant characters, always in the thick of the action and Jolie said that she was 'very social [on the film], because that's the way Lisa is. I had people in my trailer the whole time. I was like the band leader. We had crazy balloon animals and stuff and I just wanted to organise the party.'

Most of the film was shot at various locations in Harrisburg, Pennsylvania (especially Harrisburg State Hospital, whose grounds resembled those of McLean), and at weekends Jolie would get some of her co-stars in her car – including Brittany Murphy, who played the laxative abuser Daisy, and Elisabeth Moss, who played the self-harming Polly – and take them to New York. 'I got very close to some of the other girls,' said Jolie. 'Quite a few of the women on the film were with girlfriends or had female lovers or were bisexual. Probably one of the few straight women on the set was Winona.'

Whether her co-stars were as intimidated by 'band leader' Jolie as their characters were by Lisa is unknown, but one thing's for sure: they definitely knew that they had an Oscar-winning performance in their midst. According to Elisabeth Moss, 'She would walk on set and change the energy of the room. It was as if a tiger was prowling around. We all knew while we were filming that she was doing something extraordinary.'

67

When asked if Ryder was threatened by her talent and larger-than-life persona, Jolie said, 'I don't think Winona was intimidated by me. But maybe she thought I was going to try and kiss her!'

As Lisa, who Jolie said was both a 'freeing' and 'frightening' character, the actress found herself letting go and acting on her instincts. 'I thought it was going to be very hard (playing Lisa) and many parts of it were,' she said. 'But the thing is that her impulses are completely free, so I found my impulses were completely free. And my impulses are a little weird!'

Some might consider her covering the walls of her trailer in pornographic pictures a 'weird impulse' but Mangold knew exactly what Jolie was trying to get at, saying, 'Angie was just playing at living in Lisa's skin and pushing buttons any time there was a button to press. Angie is that way. She's a provocative person.'

Although Angelina described Lisa as someone who 'lived too big, was too honest, too hungry, was too full of life', it was clear that she didn't actually view any of these qualities as negative aspects of her personality. In fact, they were words she could easily have used to describe herself. While she was well aware that Lisa's antagonistic nature and menacing qualities were often destructive, not only to herself but also to her contemporaries, Angelina truly believed that her character was 'a really positive force... as someone deserving of compassion'.

While researching the role, Jolie visited a bookshop and asked the assistant to point her in the right direction for literature on sociopaths. She was mortified when the assistant told her to 'look under serial killers', for, having just made *The Bone Collector*, she knew that there was a huge difference between someone who was a killer and someone who had a personality that wasn't classed as 'normal'. 'I realised that it wasn't that people like her are haunted by dark forces,' said Jolie. 'It's just that they have certain instincts. What it comes down to is that Lisa doesn't think there's anything wrong with her. And I don't think there's anything wrong with me, but I can get angry at things and feel like it's all right just to want to live. I thought Lisa was emotional and unhappy, but she's considered psychotic and a tough woman. For me, this film wasn't about studying mental patients but just studying and enjoying life.'

Jolie may have thought the film was about 'enjoying life', but, after filming had finished, she realised that she had taken her preparation for the film too far and lost so much weight that she was horrifyingly thin. Although the role didn't require Angelina to be skeletal, she said nervous energy, which she had in abundance, had taken its toll on her body and made her lose weight. 'I'm trying to put weight on,' said the actress after *Girl, Interrupted*. 'This has been a really tough time in my life. Getting nervous, I don't eat much, even though I remind myself. And just, like, five pounds will look so different.' The actress hinted that she worried about becoming anorexic when she admitted, 'I'm hoping to get on a programme soon. I would love to have my figure back. I always felt like I didn't have one.'

Hugely defensive of her character and having invested so much in her, Jolie was shocked and upset when she saw the final cut of the film and felt that Mangold had edited out the more vulnerable side of Lisa's personality and subsequently made her a less sympathetic character. 'At the end of the film, there's a certain sense of them saying to Lisa, "Nobody wants you to live, nobody likes the way you are – you'd be better off if you were sedated and tied down and shut up." If you feel like you're the kind of person she is, then it's really hard, because you're struggling with "Fuck, am I just damaging to people everywhere? Am I just too wild and too loud and do I just need to let everybody live their lives and shut up and calm down?" If sane is thinking there's something wrong with being different, then I'd rather be completely fucking mental.' And perhaps because she saw so much of herself in Rowe, Angelina felt most affronted by the fact that by the end of the film we are led to believe that a mental institution is the only place for someone like Lisa. 'I hate to think that it's seen as right for people like her to be locked up.'

She also hated the fact that Lisa was seen as such a sexual predator when it was in fact Ryder's character who actually had sex in the film. 'People kept writing that Lisa's sexual, although I don't touch anyone. Whereas Winona's character has sex with a whole bunch of people but no one accuses her of being "sexual".'

Jolie had always been quite open about the fact that she saw most of her roles as some kind of therapy, and she hinted that playing Lisa was just another way for her to learn about herself. 'I'm not sure if this acting is something I really need to do,' said Jolie, 'or something that is coinciding in a positive way with my growing up.'

Mangold confirmed Jolie's theory when he said, 'It was clear to me I was watching someone who was not acting. There was someone speaking through her. It was a part of herself.'

As it turned out, Jolie wasn't the only one who hated the way the film turned out, and Susanna Kaysen was also quick to criticise Mangold, saying that he had taken 'Hollywood liberties' when it came to the script and plot. One example of this takes place in the scene where Lisa and Susanna escape from the hospital as part of their quest to find jobs at Disney World. This was entirely fictional and Kaysen felt as though Mangold had compromised her book in order to make the film more box-office friendly. She was, however, more than impressed with Winona's performance, which delighted Ryder. She was so attached to the film that she described it as the 'child of her heart', and to have the blessing of the author that she so admired was a huge relief.

As well as gaining the approval of Kaysen, Ryder (who

had been nominated for Oscars previously for her roles in *Little Women* and *The Age of Innocence*) was keen to impress the Academy with her portrayal of the troubled Susanna. But it was clear that it was Jolie's performance that had made the biggest impact. Ryder was overlooked, while Jolie was nominated for the Best Actress in a Supporting Role award along with Toni Collette (*The Sixth Sense*), Catherine Keener (*Being John Malkovich*), Chloë Sevigny (*Boys Don't Cry*) and Samantha Morton (*Sweet and Lowdown*). Given that Ryder had been working on getting *Girl, Interrupted* made for four years before the project got off the ground, her absence from the nominations list may well have hurt, particularly as she and Angelina weren't particularly fond of each other. However, even she couldn't have argued that Jolie didn't deserve the nod from the Academy, for her performance is compelling and it's easy to ignore Ryder's character when Jolie is on screen. While Ryder is perfectly capable as the much more introverted Susanna, she is totally overwhelmed by Jolie's ferocious and invigorating performance. As Lisa, Jolie prowls around the hospital wards like an animal seeking prey; you simply can't take your eyes off her. The film may have opened to mixed reviews, but the critics were unanimous when it came to declaring Angelina's performance an absolute triumph.

When Oscar night came, Jolie looked suitably vampish in a floor-length long-sleeved black gown and took her beloved brother James along as her 'gorgeous accessory'. Afterwards, she described 27 March as 'a beautiful day. I spent that morning with my friends, who helped me get ready, and my family came over. They told me it didn't matter one way or the other and that they loved me and were proud of me. It was the greatest day of my life already.'

If it was the greatest day of her life before she won, Jolie must have felt positively euphoric when James Coburn (who had won Best Supporting Actor the year previously for *Affliction*) called out her name as the winner in the Best Actress in a Supporting Role category.

Clearly overwhelmed by the occasion, Jolie got up from her seat – but what followed would overshadow her win entirely and be the talk of Tinseltown for months to come. As she stood up, Jolie reached over to her brother to kiss him, but, instead of giving him the obligatory Hollywood air kiss, Angelina's mouth met Jamie's and the siblings shared a kiss that looked more suitable for lovers than for a brother and sister. This possibly wouldn't have caused as much furore as it did if Angelina hadn't then declared how much she was 'in love' with her brother in her acceptance speech. As she reached the podium, an overawed Jolie gushed, 'God, I'm so surprised no one's ever fainted up here. I'm in shock. And I'm so in love with my brother right now. He just held me and said he loved me. And I know he's so happy for me… Winona, you're amazing. And Whoopi, everybody. [I'd like to thank] My family for loving me. Geyer Kosinski [her manager], my mom who's the most brave, beautiful woman I've ever known. And my dad, you're a great actor, but you're a better father. And Jamie, I have nothing without you. You're the most amazing man I've ever known and I love you.'

This luvvieness was all fairly standard fare for an overemotional Oscar-winning actress, but the comments about Jamie, coupled with that kiss, meant that Jolie's Oscar triumph was quickly transformed by the media into an incest scandal. Because she'd always been so open about experimenting with her sexuality and because she was generally considered to have a bit of a dark side, as far as the press was concerned, there was no end of possible motives for this latest move on her part. Stories abounded that she really was in love with her brother, that they were secretly sleeping together. For the first time in her life, Jolie was incredibly shocked and upset that her words and actions could have been so misunderstood.

Up until this point she'd struggled to care what anyone thought of her and her unconventional ways and, if anything, went out of her way to go against the grain and be provocative. The suggestion that she was involved with her brother in a romantic or sexual way, however, was a step too far, even for the blood-sucking Angelina, and afterwards she was appalled at the fuss that her behaviour on Oscar night caused.

'I didn't snog my brother,' said Jolie. 'I wanted an Oscar my whole life – my father had had one. Me and my brother had a very difficult upbringing. We survived a lot together and it meant a lot that he supported me my whole life. And in that moment you reach to kiss somebody and you end up kissing their mouth. Who cares? It wasn't like we had our mouths open, it wasn't some romantic kiss.'

She described the media's response as a 'crazy reaction' and said, 'I think it's pretty sad that, if you say something like that, it's interpreted in a sick way. I once thought that maybe I should play it smart and just answer questions in the slick, professional way a lot of people do. But then I realised that I'd hate myself if I did that because I didn't want to present a false image to the world.' She was also more than a little disappointed that her Oscar win had been completely overshadowed by the incident, commenting, 'For some reason, people thought it was more interesting to focus on something that was sick and disturbing rather than the fact that two siblings support and love each other. The thing is, if I were sleeping with my brother, I would tell people. People know that about me.'

From the time that Angelina and Jamie's father had left them when they were one and three respectively, the pair had been unfeasibly close, and it was only to be expected that the boy who got his little sister to perform in front of his camera as soon as she could walk and talk would want to support her on the most important night of her career. Although they were confident in their love and they knew that they hadn't done anything weird or wrong, Jolie admitted that, in the aftermath of the press frenzy, they started to question everything. 'We talked about it,' said Jolie. 'Do people actually think we're sleeping together? No, it can't possibly be. He loves movies, my brother. He knows who won every Oscar. And he was so supportive. So when I said, "I'm so in love with my brother right now," what I was trying to say was more than getting a fucking award, I can't believe how much this person loves me. If you're in a divorced family, sometimes kids get a lot closer and hold on to each other.'

Unfortunately for Angelina, James was deeply affected by the press speculation and all the negative attention made him so paranoid that he found it difficult to remain close to his sister in case it further fuelled the incest rumours. 'It has put a distance between us,' said Jolie shortly after the Oscars. 'Jamie feels he has to keep a space between us. I haven't talked to him for a few months. I think he – I'm not sure – but somehow he made a decision to not be around me so much, so we wouldn't have to answer stupid questions.'

If this wasn't distressing enough, Jolie was also concerned about how her parents would cope with the fact that people were speculating that she and James were enjoying an unnatural fling. At this stage in their mercurial relationship, Jolie and Voight were enjoying a period of closeness and, as all dads should, Voight gave his daughter some wise words. 'He's taught me that success and fame in Hollywood doesn't fulfil you,' said Jolie. 'I've never thought for a second that if I do a hit movie and I'm accepted then I'm just going to be feeling really good and everything will be OK.' Never a truer word was spoken. While she was being professionally rewarded, Jolie found herself being personally assaulted, but, as usual, the actress decided that the only way to survive in this world was to be true to herself. 'I've figured out that I can only live one way and that's to live an honest life. I'm willing to live with whatever response I get from being that way.'

Incest-gate may have ruined Jolie's Oscar night, but the cast of *Original Sin*, the film she was making in Mexico at the time of winning the award, were sure as hell going to give Jolie something to smile about when she was reunited with them. Like the true workaholic that she is, she was back on the set of the film, which also starred Antonio Banderas, the day after the Academy Awards and woke up early in the morning to find a mariachi band playing outside her trailer. The director of *Original Sin* was Michael Cristofer, with whom she had worked on *Gia*, and most of the production crew were the same team who Angelina had worked with on the film about the tragic supermodel. Having worked so closely together on two productions, they were a very tight-knit group and her colleagues were understandably proud of Jolie's achievements. While the band played, each and every one of the crew, including Banderas, stood outside Jolie's trailer and presented her with a single red rose. Jolie ended up with over 200 roses in her arms and was thrilled with their kind gesture.

'Everybody was emotional,' said Jolie. 'It was kind of like I was their little girl. And I felt like the little girl was going to survive, maybe, this business. I'd been very fragile with all of them [on *Gia*]... they knew me when I was really, really worried that I would just die young and have very little life. So it was amazing.'

Angelina's role in *Original Sin* – which was based on the novel *Waltz Into Darkness* by Cornell Woolrich – was that of a femme fatale named Julia Russell. Banderas played Luis Vargas, a wealthy Cuban businessman who sought out a mail-order bride from America (Russell) only to fall hopelessly in love with her and ultimately suffer at the hands of her scheming and manipulative ways. Jolie was perfectly cast as the beautiful and seductive con artist who, after falling in love with Vargas, finds herself at the centre of a moral dilemma.

By this stage in her career, Angelina was no stranger to starring in panned productions – which was just as well, for this time the criticism came in droves. *Original Sin* was described variously as 'dull' and 'languid' and 'never convincingly passionate nor compellingly interesting'. For something that wasn't 'convincingly passionate', the sex scenes in the film certainly caused quite a stir, particularly when stills which had been cut in the final edit were printed in the press. After viewing the steamy sex scenes between

Jolie and Banderas, producers decided to cut ten minutes' worth for fear of their explicit nature putting off potential film-goers.

Pairing Jolie with someone like Banderas was always going to end in fireworks, but no one had accounted for quite how raunchy things would get. According to the actors it was all part of the performance, and both Jolie and Banderas went out of their way to point out how unenjoyable love scenes are. 'It's not an easy thing to do,' said Banderas. 'I don't go in there thinking, "How fantastic, I am going to spend the rest of the afternoon on top of Angelina Jolie!" For both of us, it was a working day… Personally, I don't even get aroused.'

To be fair to Banderas, his lack of enjoyment probably had a lot to do with the fact that his wife, Melanie Griffiths, may have felt somewhat threatened by the beautiful, not to mention younger, Jolie. 'She is one of the most beautiful, sexy women in the world. How could you not feel funny?' Griffiths said of her husband's co-star.

As much as the media played up to this statement and speculated wildly that Jolie and Banderas were involved with each other, Melanie had nothing to worry about. In a deliberately controversial statement, Jolie insisted that, if she were to have an affair with anyone, it would be Melanie, not her husband. 'Antonio is married to a beautiful woman,' said Jolie. 'I'd sooner sleep with her than him.' And, although she admitted that there was a great 'chemistry' between her and Banderas, she too said that sex scenes looked a lot more sensual on screen than they were in real life. 'When you're shooting love scenes, there's nothing romantic or sexual about it,' said Jolie. 'It's like a weird dance. You're not exposing yourself to each other, you're not feeling the other person, and you're not really intimate. You're just pretending to be.' Jolie also claimed that she would never get involved with a married man. 'When I know someone is married with kids, it's like they're wearing some funny mask,' she said. 'They're just not a sexual person to me because I think that's so beautiful.'

Banderas was no stranger to having strong women in his life, but even he admitted that he was intimidated by Jolie's reputation. In fact, until he actually met her in person, he thought that working with her had the potential to be problematic. 'I was a little bit afraid,' he admitted. 'I survived Madonna in *Evita* and suddenly I hear I am working with Angelina. She has a reputation for being a seriously tough lady. So, I arrived on set a little bit early because I wanted to have a talk with her, but in the event I found her vulnerable and sweet. Her toughness is clearly a protective mechanism.'

Jolie was equally complimentary about her co-star, and revealed that, by the end of filming, she saw Banderas as family. 'We got to know each other quite well. He's like a strange brother. He's a sweetheart, but we're just buddies.'

While the world's media were busy making a fuss of Jolie's

close relationship with her brother and passionate sex scenes with Banderas, Jolie had very quietly fallen in love, and the press couldn't have been more wrong about where her affections lay. 'It was very obvious that this girl was in love,' said Banderas of his *Original Sin* co-star. But who exactly was this secret lover?

chapter 7

the crazy world of
billy bob

Angelina may have been publicly declaring her love for her brother on Oscar night, but at the time there was another man she just couldn't get out of her mind. After she had accepted her award, the first thing she did was make a phone call, desperately trying to reach the man she'd been secretly in love with for months. This man was Billy Bob Thornton, whom Angelina had met on the set of *Pushing Tin* in 1998, and, as soon as she had made an obligatory appearance at the post-Oscar parties, Jolie headed straight to the Sunset Marquis hotel, where Thornton was staying. When she arrived, Billy Bob was in his pyjamas, having just put his sons William and Harry to bed, and he and Angelina sat in the grounds of the hotel and talked about her victory. This may sound like a low-key celebration for an actress who had just been honoured by the Academy, but all

Angelina cared about at this moment in time was being with Billy Bob. And, if that had meant travelling to the end of the earth, she would have done it.

In fact, she had to get up at 4am the next morning to fly to Mexico, where she was filming *Original Sin* with Antonio Banderas, but lack of sleep was not something this love-struck actress cared about.

Although they met on the set of *Pushing Tin*, Angelina and Billy Bob had shared a manager, Geyer Kosinski, for years, and he had told them about each other, knowing that they were likely to hit it off. He once told Thornton, 'There's this girl, and she's kind of like you as an actor. She's the female you. I'm afraid to introduce you because I'm afraid you'll get married.'

In fact, before Jolie and Thornton ever spoke to each other, they had been in the same room but Angelina had actively avoided the actor, possibly because she was intimidated by her manager's prediction. There was no room for avoidance, however, when she encountered him again in an elevator in Toronto, shortly after arriving there to film *Pushing Tin*. According to both Jolie and Thornton, after seeing each other in that lift, they both knew that their lives would never be the same again.

In an interview with *Rolling Stone* magazine, both recounted the moment they first laid eyes on each other with characteristic honesty, and Thornton revealed his opening gambit. 'I said, "I'm Billy Bob, how are you doing?" And I just remember... you know, wanting something to not go away. Wishing the elevator had gone to China. It's like a bolt of lightning. Something happened that never happened before.'

Jolie was equally bowled over by his presence, reflecting, 'Something went wrong with me in the elevator. Chemical. I really walked into a wall. I kind of knocked [the elevator] as we were both getting out. He got into a van and said, "I'm trying on some pants – you want to come?" And I nearly passed out. All I heard was him and taking off his pants. I just said no. And then I went round the corner and sat against a wall, breathing, thinking, "What... was... that?' Jesus, how am I going to work?" I became a complete idiot.'

If anything, this incident probably helped Jolie get into the character of Mary Bell, who is the somewhat obsessed wife of Thornton's character Russell Bell in *Pushing Tin*. The film looks at the lives of a group of New York-based air-traffic controllers, led by Nick Falzone (played by John Cusack), who are shaken up by the arrival of the new kid in town, Russell Bell. While Cusack is perfectly cast as the neurotic and self-obsessed Nick, Thornton was made for the part of the enigmatic and elusive loner, Russell. Newell had every confidence that Angelina would more than hold her own as the beautiful yet disturbed Mary, saying, 'Angelina has the acting gift and the camera is in love with her.'

Jolie had originally been lined up to play Connie Falzone but turned it down because she didn't feel that she knew enough about being a mother and the part eventually went to Cate Blanchett. She is, however, fantastic as Russell's wife who is constantly craving her husband's attention and you could say it was a case of life imitating art when Jolie found herself spellbound by Thornton in the lift that day.

Although the attraction between these two was undeniably instant, they didn't get together for several months after first meeting. Thornton was living with and engaged to the actress Laura Dern (they met on the set of *Ellen* while filming the 'Coming Out' episode in March 1997) at the time, and although Jolie had enjoyed a year-long relationship with Timothy Hutton after splitting from Jonny Lee Miller, her divorce from the actor was still not finalised. They became close throughout filming, nonetheless, and often went out to dinner, although never alone. 'We would say strange things. We would just randomly be talking about something in our lives, like the difficulty of living with people, and he'd say, "I could live with you,"' said Jolie.

Angelina knew in her head that they 'were not able to be together at that time', but Billy Bob had stolen her heart, and shortly after meeting him she had a tattoo of his name done in her groin area to celebrate the fact that she had found someone so special. (Billy Bob would not know of this tattoo's existence until much later.) Despite the simmering sexual tension between the two, they were consummate professionals on set and, according to the producer Art

Linson, 'They were extremely convincing as a couple in front of the camera but I thought it was just real good acting and nothing more.'

And they certainly did not declare themselves to each other at this time, with Thornton admitting afterwards, 'We never said one day we're going to be together. But I know now that it was impossible not to be together.'

As show business gossip tries to romantically link Jolie to every man she ever works with, it seems strange that no one suspected the romance between Jolie and Thornton, but, perhaps because of the 20-year age gap and Thornton's involvement with Dern, nobody gave their friendship a second thought. When asked how they managed to keep it all under wraps, Jolie remarked that 'nobody was looking for it'.

After they had finished *Pushing Tin*, Jolie and Thornton had a few months with no contact, but eventually their close friendship resumed via the telephone. When they did finally get together, however, the relationship was not without its dramas. In fact, just days before their Las Vegas wedding on 5 May 2000, Jolie was sectioned and spent 72 hours in UCLA's Medical Center after experiencing 'paralysing grief' and 'suicidal' thoughts about the fact the she couldn't have Billy Bob.

Angelina later described the series of events to *Rolling Stone* magazine: 'What happened is, we didn't know if we were going to be able to be together. I remember him driving somewhere and not knowing if he was OK... We had wanted to get married and then, for all the different reasons, we thought we couldn't. And I, for some reason, thought something had happened to him and I lost the ability to... I just went a little insane.'

The irony of the fact that Jolie had just won an Oscar for playing a girl in a psychiatric hospital was not lost on the actress. 'Trust me, it was funny, looking back. It must have thrown those girls [in the hospital] for a loop. I was stuttering, out of my mind, and they'd seen me playing the part in a movie. Very strange. I got involved with them. One listened constantly to depressing suicide music. I wanted to make her feel better so I left her my Walkman with some Clash, and aggressive fighting tunes.'

Although many could see Jolie as a bad role model in the sense that she's been open about her drug taking, her self-harm and her obsession with blood, there is something to be said for an actress who is willing to bare her soul in the way that she does. One thing she feels strongly about is honesty, and, as far as she's concerned, only good things can come from her revealing details about such incidents as her breakdown. 'I don't mind showing my flaws. It helps other girls realise they can survive. I live strong, love strong, do everything strong. I'm a therapist's dream.'

Just before the breakdown, Jolie had been visiting Thornton in Nashville. When her mum went to the airport in LA to pick up her daughter, Angelina 'couldn't stop crying' and was in a state of severe distress. Doing what all mothers would do in this situation, Bertrand sought professional advice and, within hours, Angelina was taken to hospital. Doctors likened her behaviour to that of someone who was grieving and Jolie admits that at this stage she thought Billy Bob 'was gone' and reasoned, 'Maybe part of me needed to shut down for a few days to process everything before; I don't know.'

Despite her daughter's protestations to the contrary, Marcheline thought the only solution was to track Thornton down and tell him about what was happening. Subsequently, within hours of Jolie being discharged, Jolie and Thornton were married.

While it was Angelina's second marriage, it was Billy Bob's fifth. And no one was more surprised, not to mention distraught, at the news of the wedding than Laura Dern, who was unaware that her relationship with Thornton was over. Only the previous October, Thornton had spoken of how happy he was with her, saying, 'I am happily involved with someone who's my best friend. We have a dog and a yard.'

They may have had a dog and a yard, but their relationship was clearly lacking in communication. According to Dern, 'I left home to work on a movie and while I was away my boyfriend got married and I've never heard from him again. It's like a sudden death.'

Like Jolie, Thornton had never been one to do things by

halves when it came to love. Born in Hot Springs, Arkansas, on 4 August 1955, Thornton was 20 years older than Jolie, but the age difference was of no relevance to the pair, who felt like they were soulmates. 'Age doesn't mean a thing to me,' said Jolie. 'I was once married to a man my own age and it didn't work out.'

Their backgrounds were quite different too. Jolie grew up among showbiz royalty. Thornton grew up 'in the woods' with his mother Virginia, who was a psychic (she predicted that her son would work with Burt Reynolds and win an Oscar, both of which came true – Thornton went on to the write *The Gift*, based on his mother), his father Billy Ray, a high-school history teacher and basketball coach, and his two younger brothers John David and Jimmy Don. The couple bonded, however, over their mutual feeling of not belonging anywhere. They were both tortured souls who often felt misunderstood and finding each other finally made them feel at ease with the world. 'I never thought I'd be calm or settled or satisfied,' said Jolie. 'I thought I only lived, like, five per cent alive and I can't do this any more and I'll never stay in one place and no one will ever really get inside me and I feel kind of empty. And now I'm completely calm and I feel I have so much meaning in my life and I'm so clear. He's just made me complete. I just admire him and have so much fun with him.' She also credited her husband with teaching her how to love and accept herself, something she had clearly struggled to do in her darker periods. 'We didn't belong anywhere 'til we met each other. We understand each other completely. I didn't even know how to love myself until Billy taught me what love is.'

Thornton was equally complimentary about the effect Angelina had had on his life, saying, 'She saved my soul. I was on my way out. I was living a lie I didn't belong in. I was drowning in sadness. Angelina, she lifted me up.'

And despite his previous four marriages – he married Melissa Gaitlin in 1978, with whom he has a daughter Amanda Spence; was married to the actress Toni Lawrence between 1986 and 1988; married another actress Cynda William in 1990; and he then went on to have two sons with his fourth wife Pietra Dawn Cherniak, whom he was with from 1993 to 1997 – Billy Bob was more than confident that it was a case of fifth time lucky. 'You spend your whole life saying, "This is it", "This is it", "This is it",' said Thornton. 'And, when it really is it, you're like the boy who cried wolf. But this really is, it really is.'

Cynics doubted from the start that the Thornton–Jolie union would be a lasting one, but Thornton was quick to defend his actions. 'Look, we can't prove to you that we're going to stay together forever, but we just are. Five years later, we'll meet again and you'll go, "How's your wife?" and I'll go, "She's just fine." In the past I was never in the right spot, that's all. And you know what? When you finally get where you're supposed to be, that's great.'

Billy Bob certainly matched Angelina in the eccentricity

department, and, while she was quite open about her collection of knives, he was famous for his Obsessive Compulsive Disorder, phobia of antiques and penchant for orange foods. Both actors had also experienced difficult relationships with their fathers, with Thornton admitting that his father was a 'monster' who 'never really liked me'. As with Angelina, it was Billy Bob's strong will that caused problems in the relationship with his father: 'They say he was crazy about me when I was a baby. But, when I started talking, it was all over. He didn't like anyone with their own opinions.'

With this in mind, there can be no doubt that, among other things, he and Angelina bonded over issues with their respective fathers.

Thornton, like Jolie, had experimented with drugs in his youth, but had also put a stop to it before it was too late. 'You can make decisions. You're not an idiot. I look at my kids and think, "I'm not going anywhere."' In 2001, he revealed, 'I haven't had alcohol for about six years. And it's been 20 years since I've been on drugs. I mean, you just feel better, period.' He even went as far as to quit smoking, when Angelina had to give up in preparation for her role as Lara Croft in *Tomb Raider*. A further inspiration was the fact that his father had died of lung cancer when Billy was only 18 years old.

Although Angelina would be the first to balk at the idea of getting on in Hollywood thanks to nepotism, there can be no doubt that her famous connections helped her to get a foot in the door. While she maintains that she went to auditions without telling directors who her father was, growing up with a film-star dad would at the very least have shown her which doors to knock on. Billy Bob had no such luxury, and, when he and a childhood friend, Tom Epperson, moved to LA in 1991, they struggled for years to make it in Tinseltown. At one point, the cash-deprived Billy went so long without food that he was admitted to hospital with malnutrition. Luckily for him, his doctor was from Arkansas and let him stay for a whole week even though he had no medical insurance.

Like most actors, Thornton, who was also a musician and was in a soul group called Blue and the Blue Velvets, had the obligatory dead-end jobs before making it big, and it was when he was working as a waiter at an industry event that he bumped into Billy Wilder, who, after speaking to him for a while, advised him to try his hand at screenwriting. Thornton took his advice and wrote *One False Move* (1992) with Epperson and then *Sling Blade* (1996) which he wrote, directed and starred in. *Sling Blade* was the story of the mentally handicapped Karl Childers, who, having killed his mother and his lover at the age of 12, is released from a psychiatric hospital as an adult and has to readjust to life in his hometown. The film got Thornton the recognition that he'd been praying for from the movie industry: he was nominated for the Best Actor award at the

1996 Academy Awards and walked away with the Oscar for Best Adapted Screenplay.

Angelina was totally in awe of Billy Bob from the moment they met – something that had a lot to do with his creativity. She once remarked that she ended up with men she wanted to be, and, in Billy's case, she very much saw him as an artist. Soon after their wedding, Billy wrote two songs for the actress, 'Your Blue Shadow' and 'Angelina', and his wife was clearly in awe of his talent and overwhelmed by the gesture. 'I'll never forget the first time she heard "Angelina". When I played it to her, man, she just cried. Every line means something to us that no one will ever know and, well, it can be emotional. It's the same with "Your Blue Shadow". Anyone hearing the songs can work out what it's about but the lines have a deeper meaning for both of us.'

It wouldn't be unreasonable to think that Angelina was downgrading when she hooked up with Billy Bob. After all, she is possibly the most beautiful and lusted-after actress in the world, while he is a scrawny Southerner who – well, looks a bit rough round the edges. However, this is a man who oozes sexuality and has an undeniably magnetic quality. His co-star in *Monster's Ball* said of his appeal, 'He's very sexy. I think he's handsome, absolutely. But his sex appeal comes from something else – the way he looks at you, the way he takes you in.'

Although Angelina was undoubtedly more than a match for her husband in the sexiness stakes, the actress really didn't think she was in his league. Sounding like a schoolgirl with a crush, Jolie said shortly after their wedding, 'I didn't think I was good enough for Billy and I'm honoured to be with him. He stands for all the things I stand for, he and I live by the same code of ethics. We also have the same sense of humour, the same dreams, the same wishes. I still can't believe he married me!'

Their wedding – somewhat predictably – was not of the most traditional nature. Although it wasn't quite as bizarre as Angelina's first, it wasn't exactly a church-and-vicar affair either. Jolie's bridal attire comprised of jeans and a sleeveless blue sweater, while Thornton also wore jeans and one of his trademark baseball caps. The $189 'Beginning Package' ceremony took place in the Little Church of the West Wedding Chapel in Las Vegas on 5 May 2000, and Jolie did stick to two marital traditions by carrying red and white roses and walking down the aisle to 'Here Comes the Bride'. The service was short (20 minutes long, to be exact) and sweet and Jolie promised to love and honour Thornton, though not to obey him. The witness and best man at the ceremony was Thornton's friend, the cinematographer Harvey Cook, who had worked with Thornton on *All The Pretty Horses*. Although none of Angelina's family was present, it's thought that they approved of her new relationship. James had helped her pack her things to go off to New York and, with regard to her father, Angelina said, 'My dad knew there was someone in my life because he saw how happy I was, so he couldn't help but be very pleased about it.'

Voight, however, sounded a bit more hesitant about the whole thing. 'They stick by each other and care deeply for each other. You're always going through things with young people and hoping they'll come out the other side. Hopefully she'll not do anything she can't recover from.' Perhaps he had the same reservations about the relationship as the rest of the world, but was just too afraid to say it. After all, it must have been frightening for him to see his daughter fall so hard for someone who had been through four wives already.

The duo started as they meant to go on, and for the duration of their marriage they were considered to be the most eccentric and unconventional couple in Hollywood. And, given how open they were about their life in interviews, this is hardly surprising. At any given opportunity, they would gush about their undying love for each other and at times it sounded almost too good to be true. 'We love each other obsessively, madly,' said Jolie.

'We stalk each other round the house,' con-firmed Thornton.

They were also incredibly frank about their sex life – something that the media is not used to dealing with when it comes to A-list celebrities. Angelina would tell interviewers that she had 'rug burns' from having sex on their pool table at home, that they were 'addicted to each other' and that 'Billy's an amazing lover and he knows my body. He does certain things to me in bed that, well, they're beautiful. He can make me calm and happy.'

Thornton was no less discreet, revealing, 'Every time we do it, it gets more and more exciting.'

One reporter in particular got more than he bargained for when he stopped Billy Bob and Angelina on the red carpet of the MTV Awards 2000, and asked them, 'What's the most exciting thing you guys have ever done in a car?'

Billy Bob shrugged his shoulders in a nonchalant fashion and said, 'We just fucked in the car.'

There could be no doubt that their sex life was intense. So intense, in fact, that they described their desire for each other as almost violent. 'I was looking at her asleep and literally had to restrain myself from squeezing her to death. Sex for us is almost too much. It's so intense that sometimes we can look at each other and think, "We can't get into this right now or something's going to happen."'

Rather than being scared by this sentiment, Angelina was thrilled. 'You know when you love someone so much you can almost kill them? I nearly was killed one night, and it's the nicest thing anyone's ever said to me.' She then stated that she wanted to 'eat his earlobe' and that she'd 'kill anyone who even looked at him the wrong way'.

They bought their first home, rather appropriately, from rock 'n' roll legend Slash (the Guns 'N' Roses guitarist), one of its main attractions being that it had a basement in which

Billy Bob could record his music. Voight helped his daughter move in and it wasn't long before their walls were adorned with framed poems that he had written for them. Despite his fears for Angelina, he was clearly willing to hope for the best and wish the couple well.

As you would expect, the Jolie–Thornton household was adorned with an array of bizarre ornaments. On a shopping trip to Harrods, Angelina bypassed the designer clothes and headed straight for the toy department, where she ordered a life-size horse for the house. The idea was that she would order five of them so they could have people round to watch TV while sitting on the horses. The couple also had a collection of *King of the Hill* DVDs and they liked nothing more than ordering in from Angelina's favourite takeaway place – Why Cook? – and watching episodes of the show in bed.

She and Billy bought a rat, which they named Harry, and a myna bird named Alice. While Billy Bob would spend hours trying to teach Alice to say 'Fuck You', Angelina would entertain the rat, which lived in a cage less than three feet from the end of their bed. 'Billy found me one day sitting in the bathtub in my pyjamas, the rat on my lap, feeding it pumpkin pie. See, that's one of those things that only someone who really loves me is going to think is cute.'

Such was the importance of these animals in their household that, when Angelina and Billy Bob renewed their vows in their house with a woman from the Church of

Enlightenment, she mentioned 'four-footed Harry and winged Alice' in the ceremony. Renewing their vows was something that this couple planned to do 'every now and then' according to Thornton, presumably so they could reaffirm their love for each other. During this particular ceremony, they didn't so much exchange rings as each cut their fingers and suck each other's blood, but, before anyone had time to register shock, Jolie insisted that it was 'very sweetly done'.

Thornton even joked that one day they would have a role reversal where 'I'm going to be the bride and she'll be the groom. She's got me these pink panties with a big bow on them.'

On one occasion, Thornton was actually caught wearing his wife's underwear in his local gym, while she was off filming *Tomb Raider* in England. 'I thought they were hidden,' said Thornton, 'but some guy kept looking at me strange. I said, "They're my wife's."' He also admitted that he wore them on the set of *Bandits* (the film he made with Bruce Willis) some days, just to keep his wife 'close to him'.

His wife actively encouraged such behaviour and admitted, 'The fact is, I like to see him in every different way and one of them being, yeah, in my underwear.'

Billy Bob had his own ideas when it came to his wife's attire and bought her a selection of outfits, including a tutu and a Red Riding Hood outfit. Although she admitted that she 'liked costumes', she revealed that what she actually wore round the house most of the time wasn't so wild. 'I tend to just walk round in nightgowns and little white socks.'

Thornton's sons from his marriage to Pietra Cherniak were regular visitors to their home, and William and Harry would delight in the treats the couple would lay on for them. One journalist visited their home to do an interview only to find two tents camped out in the master bedroom, where the boys had been sleeping. Billy Bob also had the inspired idea of creating a Velcro room for the boys to play in. 'The Velcro room is because we have two little boys who like to play,' he explained. 'You put a suit on, you jump on the wall, you stick. It's fun! At least we're honest about it.' The couple even planned an adult version of this and dreamed of creating a padded room so they could 'go crazy' while having sex. 'We enjoy the most intense, crazy, do-anything-you-want-to-me sex but we don't do any weird shit. We don't hurt each other, we just love each other,' said Thornton.

Angelina was the first to admit it was 'corny', but the couple also talked of having sex in the elevator inside their house, given that they had first met in one.

It was clear even at this stage that Angelina very much enjoyed exercising her maternal instinct, albeit in stepmum role. She clearly loved developing a close relationship with Billy's sons, and was more than happy for the boys to be a part of everyday life. 'Billy Bob has two beautiful children,' said Jolie. 'They're just turning seven and eight so they are still babies really. They live with their mother and she is wonderful about letting them get to know me. So we are a family already.'

Given how unhappy parts of her own childhood had been, it seemed rather as if Jolie was living vicariously through the two boys. 'I'm almost having my childhood now,' she admitted. 'I'm soft and silly and for the first time in years, with my husband and his children, I can finally be a kid.'

In November 2001, Jolie enthused about the Halloween festivities she had shared with them: 'We all dressed up as rabbits and went through these tunnels made out of boxes and ate carrots. Billy and I had full rabbit suits, like big pink pyjamas. Then we watched *Charlie Brown* and *Scooby Doo* and carved pumpkins. You had to be there. It was a whole bunch of chaos.'

It was obvious that Jolie revelled in this level of domesticity and loved the security of being part of a solid family unit. 'I used to look at houses, drive by them when I lived in apartments, and I always wanted to be in a house with a dog, having dinner, talking about your life.' Billy could do the smallest of things, yet it would bring Angelina no end of joy – like a smitten mother who is marvelling at her child being able to walk for the first time. 'We were upstairs the other day and just laughing, because we realised: we're married and this is our home. Like, we have a dishwasher. We do the simplest things, like he lights the fireplace in my office, and I'm floored, I'm so proud.' She even did the decent thing and left her knife collection back in New York when they moved into their house, so as not to put his kids in any danger. As she said herself, 'There's no place for knives when there's kids around.'

Despite the fact that she said her and Billy planned to adopt when his two boys were a bit older, Jolie also dreamed of having some of their own children. Ironically, however, she worried about the effect this would have on their relationship. 'I would love to have children with Billy, but I also know some people fall in love with their children so much that they don't put as much focus on their husband or wife. So right now I'm getting to know my husband and his children. But, if we had a child, it would be amazing.'

Little did she know that she had just predicted exactly what would go wrong in her relationship with Billy Bob.

Angelina was already planning on adoption too, and she seemed pretty confident that her husband was on board with all her hopes and dreams. She talked very much in the long term, and clearly had no doubt that the couple would fulfil all their dreams together. 'We both want to adopt more children. There are brothers and sisters who have trouble being adopted or being kept together and fortunately we are able to financially take on more than one child and keep families together. I think you find each other in this world, like lovers find each other and husbands and wives find each other and are meant to take care of each other. I've visited lots of different countries and refugee camps and I just know that, one day, we will adopt.'

One day, the couple would indeed adopt, but unfortunately it wouldn't work out quite the way Angelina had wished.

In the meantime, however, all was well with the couple and they continued to honour each other's love with hugely emotional declarations and, at times, frankly bizarre gestures. It was clear from her relationship with Jonny Lee Miller that Angelina wasn't shy when it came to saying it with blood (as opposed to flowers) and this unusual fascination continued throughout her relationship with Billy Bob. If this marriage will be remembered for anything, it will be for the fact that they wore vials of blood round each other's neck. 'Some people think a diamond is really pretty,' said Jolie. 'My husband's blood is the most beautiful thing in the world to me. There are only so many ways to say you love somebody, to say, "I would truly die for you. I want to live out my days, my life with you. I am your partner, your blood and we share the same life." It's not dark or trying to be provocative in any way.' She even admitted at one stage that, 'If there was a safe way to drink his blood, I would.'

While some husbands may have run for the hills at the thought of wearing their wife's blood as an accessory, Thornton was more than happy to embrace the eccentricity of the whole thing, saying of the vials, 'Angie got them for Christmas. We poked our fingers and we put our blood in there so when we're apart we have a little bit of each other. I wear it every day and she wears one just like it, with my blood.'

The bloody antics didn't end there, though, and for their first Christmas together Angelina used her own blood to paint 'Till The End Of Time' on a plaque above their bed – reflecting how long she felt she would love him for. On their first anniversary, Billy would return the favour and write the same words in his own blood underneath hers – and even had a nurse draw his blood so he could paint some pictures with it. Angelina went one better by presenting her husband with a box full of her blood and then, just to ensure that they really would be together forever, she celebrated their wedding anniversary by buying 'his and hers' graves next to the plot of his late brother Jimmy Don's grave in Arkansas. (Jimmy Don died of a heart condition when he was 30; Thornton says he's never really got over his death.) Billy was clearly touched by this gesture and said that the gift was 'a comfort to us both'. So extreme were their gestures that Thornton admitted there was little they could do to top them. 'What can I do next to prove my love? I guess I'm just going to have to fly up to the moon, tear it in half and hand her a piece!'

While most people scoffed at the way the duo liked to express their love, there is something undeniably romantic about the fact that none of their gifts was remotely materialistic, which was quite refreshing for two Hollywood stars. If they'd wanted to shower each other in diamonds, then it would certainly have been an option financially, but it would take more than money for these two to prove their devotion. And, ever the faithful brother, James Haven rose to Angelina's defence when her behaviour was criticised, arguing, 'If wearing blood vials keeps her calm, knowing it's going to be OK because she is going to see him again, then great. That's fantastic for her.'

For Christmas 2001, Thornton revealed that he and Jolie had set each other the challenge of making gifts. 'We've decided to give each other one thing apiece. If you knew anything about how little we know how to make, it's pretty hilarious. She's ruined a few things trying to make me something already. Like, she tried to knit a scarf and she said it was a real disaster. I think she'll like what I'm going to give her. I'm just making her a little thing. I mean, it's very simple what I'm making her. It's not weird or particularly interesting but, to her, it will be.'

One thing Angelina did manage to make successfully was a photo album, which combined pictures from Billy's childhood with some from her own, so it looked like they had grown up together.

With both stars huge fans of body art, it was only a matter of time before they had tattoos of each other's name done (although Angelina had his name tattooed on her groin when they first met, she had a more visible one done on her left arm when they officially became a couple – in fact, it was when she showed it off in public that the world first became aware of their relationship). Billy Bob had the word 'Angelina' tattooed on his left arm, with the 'L' of her name covering a vein. He then had four drops of blood tattooed on (which looked like they were coming from the vein), which were there to represent him, Angelina and his two sons. The twosome also had a mysterious script tattooed on their inner right forearms. 'It means something to us, but nobody else [can know] what it means or it breaks the spell,' explained Thornton.

On another occasion, both Angelina and Billy Bob decided to involve a notary in their actions. Jolie changed her will to say that she and Billy should be buried together and had it notarised; meanwhile, quite unaware of her actions, Billy Bob signed a piece of paper in his own blood saying they would be married for eternity – again, in front of a notary. When they told each other about what they'd done, Jolie says that they 'laughed that we had both dealt with a notary.'

Knowing how the media grab on to every sordid detail of celebrities' lives, Thornton and Jolie must have known what a furore the revelations about their personal preferences would cause, yet they seemed hurt and disappointed that their behaviour should be seen as anything out of the ordinary, and were at pains to point out how deeply 'normal' their lives really were. Billy Bob seemed quite philosophical about this and realised that it was the more freaky aspects of their lifestyle that the press would focus on.

'Angelina and I are known for being insane, but we're not really. We have a really good life. We live in a tiny world and we don't pay much attention to anything else. When you're first coming up in your career, people only want the edgy part of you, so you play it up.'

He was also quick to defend the idea that his wife was the dark and sinister person she was made out to be, saying, 'Angie's a real kind person who's doing a lot of good things in this world and I'm trying to do that too. More than anything else, we've given each other a sense of peace. We have a great home and a great life, we're both doing work we like, we support each other – and that's really what we're all about. I know it's disappointing, but we're actually more normal than people think.'

In many ways, the couple broke boundaries in Hollywood. This is the town where images are created (not to mention secrets kept) by controlling agents, managers and PRs; by being so honest about their lives, Billy Bob and Angelina were sticking two fingers up to all this. 'Society trains us to lie and hide our real thoughts and you wonder about that kind of training,' said Jolie. 'We're all so concerned about appearances that we lose sight of the truth... I've taken the risk of being open because I want to celebrate the truth and feel I have nothing to hide about my love for my husband. I want people to know how good our being together has made me feel. How can that be bad?'

It's no coincidence that, soon after parting company with

his long-term publicist Pat Kingsley, Tom Cruise appeared on Oprah Winfrey's show and jumped up and down on the sofa declaring his love for Katie Holmes. This was a side of Cruise that had never been seen before – due to the fact that, up until that point, his image had been controlled by his management.

As Jolie said, 'Love is a risk. Life is a risk.' It's just that the movers and shakers in Hollywood aren't willing to take risks if it means that audiences are put off going to see a movie because the female lead likes to suck blood in her free time.

Ironically, Billy Bob knew that the kind of love they shared is what movies are made of, but came to the conclusion that, as much as people like to see that on screen, they don't like to be confronted with it in real life. 'You know what? If someone puts it right in your face, most people don't accept it. We're going to live like it is when people go watch [movies]. Someone running through the rain, their fucking arm cut off... See, I would do that for her in real life. Some of the things we do, if we did them in a movie, people would say it was so romantic, but you do it in real life and everybody calls you a weirdo.'

Fortunately, Billy Bob never had to cut an arm off for Angelina. Unfortunately, their relationship would eventually encounter problems that couldn't be solved by a grand romantic gesture.

Chapter 8

meet lara croft

After winning an Oscar for *Girl, Interrupted*, it was thought that Angelina would go on to make more films of a serious nature, cashing in on the fact that Hollywood had taken notice of her and industry bigwigs regarded her as one of the most talented actresses of her generation. It was a surprise, therefore, when, after completing *Original Sin*, Jolie opted for roles of a less challenging nature. And *Gone in 60 Seconds* – a remake of the 1974 film of the same name – appealed to her for that very reason. 'I just came out of a mental institution with a bunch of women,' said Jolie of her time on *Girl, Interrupted*. 'Now, that was high energy and raw and tough. This was playful. It was fun being part of a team.' And if her involvement in such a project was going to do her reputation any harm, Jolie couldn't have cared less. 'I want to play a character, I want to go crazy and I want to play with cars; if that means I don't have an image as a "serious actress" then fine.'

The fact that *Gone in 60 Seconds* would allow her to work in a predominantly male environment after working with the aforementioned 'bunch of women' also hugely appealed to the actress. Jolie revealed, 'It was a script they gave me that was nothing but Ferraris, Nic Cage and Giovanni Ribisi and that sounded like a good idea. It's a fun movie and I tried just to have fun.' Always eager to learn something new, Jolie, who sports blonde dreadlocks in the film, also enjoyed the fact that she was taught how to hotwire cars for her role. Sara 'Sway' Wayland, the sexy mechanic by day and bartender by night, plays a part in the huge car heist that forms the basis of the plot and Angelina didn't want to let the side down when it came to looking like a smooth criminal. 'They really did teach us, which is great. That's one of the greatest things about my job is that you get to learn all these different skills you never thought you would.'

Despite the fact that *Gone in 60 Seconds* had a bigger opening at cinemas than any other film Jolie had starred in, it wasn't exactly a huge critical success. One reviewer noted, 'It was barely a movie at all. It was more like a thousand car commercials spliced together.'

Negative comments from critics couldn't detract from the fact that Angelina had had a ball on the set and, as always, she bonded particularly well with one of her male co-stars.

'Nic's amazing,' she said of Nicolas Cage, who played the retired car thief Randall 'Memphis' Raines in the film. 'He's a really great team leader and he supports all the other actors. He lets them do their thing. He seems very serious but he's also completely nuts and free.' Rather predictably, Jolie was romantically linked to Cage but insisted that the pair were nothing more than friends. 'He's a sweetheart. We're friends, we worked together, but no...'

She might have thought 'no', but this feeling wasn't necessarily mutual and, when Nicolas Cage later split with his wife Lisa Marie Presley, in November 2002, he allegedly sent Angelina flowers and romantic cards. The two actors were seen out on the town together, and were reported to have spent the night at one particular showbiz bash 'dancing and kissing'. They may have shared a kiss, but, at the time, Jolie was still reeling from the end of her second marriage and the fact that she had just adopted a child, so it's unlikely that her alleged involvement with Cage was very high up on her list, and no doubt his, of priorities.

Gone in 60 Seconds had given Jolie a taste for action films and her next step was to sign up for the film version of the popular computer game and comic book *Tomb Raider*. The role of archaeologist and photojournalist Lara Croft would certainly be challenging for Jolie in the physical sense but, in terms of showcasing her dramatic skills, it wasn't the most demanding of parts. Angelina, however, was quick to defend her decision to take on the persona of the female action figure, saying, 'There's this idea that, if you're an Oscar winner, you should take yourself seriously. And that's stupid. You should do what you feel like doing. Nobody should ever take themselves seriously. Period.'

Ironically, Jolie's first experience of the upper-class English heroine was not a good one. While married to Jonny Lee Miller, she had often fought for his attention as he sat glued to his computer screen, playing the *Tomb Raider* games. Like all PlayStation widows, Jolie grew to resent Lara Croft and the fact that she was competing with a computer image for attention. In fact, when she was first approached by the director Simon West to take on the role, she was appalled. 'When they called me about Lara Croft I said, "Oh, God, not her." When they asked me to play Lara, I told them they were insane. Like every woman, I rolled my eyes and thought, "I hate her."' This ill-feeling may have been fuelled by the fact that Jolie wasn't exactly adept at playing the game herself. 'I tried but I'd get frustrated. I could never get her over the wall, so I'd just throw things. I didn't hate the game, but I can't play it. I break computers.'

Despite her initial reaction, for Jolie it was a case of 'If you can't beat 'em join 'em' and before long she had signed up for the film. And, as for Simon West, he simply couldn't imagine anyone else fitting the role so perfectly. 'It was always Angelina. I mean, Lara sleeps with knives and doesn't take any shit from anybody. That's AJ down to a tee. Besides, all-out action and Angelina Jolie? What red-blooded adolescent male would say no to that? You can have thrills, spills and your first sexual experience all at the same time!'

He was right about that. She may not have been real, but Lara Croft was the ultimate pin-up for adolescent boys (and grown men, for that matter) across the world, and the thought of her being brought to life in the form of the delectable Angelina Jolie was almost too good to be true. With her long dark hair, enviable curves and no-nonsense attitude, Lara could almost have been based on Angelina. And even Jolie couldn't deny their similarities. 'I'm very loud and physical and insane so I fit into this role perfectly,' said Jolie. And of their physical similarities, she conceded that, 'The strange thing is that she actually looks like me. Our skin, our hair and our bodies are just the same. That's pretty scary.'

It wasn't so scary for the makers of the film, who delighted in the fact that they had found their girl. And they must have been relieved to have got her on board, given that, in the not so distant past, Jolie had passed up the opportunity to be part of the *Charlie's Angels* remake. Although it would be many a female actress's dream to take part in the remake of such an iconic show, the glamour of *Charlie's Angels* didn't appeal to Jolie. 'With *Charlie's Angels* I made my decision because 1) I didn't watch the original TV series and 2) I don't get dressed up. Also, I'm probably not the best group person, so it didn't really suit my personality.'

With this last comment in mind, it's easy to see how the one-woman show that is *Tomb Raider* seemed like such an attractive prospect.

There were also several aspects to Croft's character that impressed Jolie. As a child, Angelina was more likely to be playing with knives than trying out different ways to wear her hair, and, while Lara is beautiful, she certainly has a no-frills approach to dressing and spends most of her time in shorts and a tank top. In the fictional story, Lara wasn't much of a team player when she attended Gordonstoun boarding school in Scotland and favoured walking the hills alone as opposed to joining in netball practice with the other girls. She was a survivor, she was eager to learn about the world and she didn't need anyone else's help along the way. Why, the two women were like peas in a pod! And Jolie was the first to admit it. 'The things I have in common with Lara Croft are that I am good at being alone, without a man to help me, and I am a fighter. When I believe in something, I go out and get it. Lara doesn't have to dress like a boy or act like a boy to be tough. I grew up loving Sophia Loren and these kinds of women and I love that Lara is a tough woman. It's great to be that empowered.'

These girls might not need a man to help them get by, but, for the duration of filming, Jolie was pining for the husband she was so helplessly in love with. In fact, the reason she and Thornton married so soon after getting together was that Angelina knew she was going to be absent for months and the couple wanted to do something to put a more serious stamp on their relationship. 'We knew there would never be anyone else in our lives,' said Jolie. 'But I was going to shoot *Tomb Raider* in England and we decided that we didn't just want to be boyfriend and girlfriend any more.' The actress was also amused by the fact that, in a period in her life when she was playing such a headstrong, independent woman, she was at her most smitten. 'It's funny that my toughest role should come at the time when I'm feeling my most soft. It's really quite ironic.'

She may have been feeling soft on the inside, but Jolie was more than prepared to throw herself into what ended up being months of physical preparation for the role. As someone who had a very unhealthy lifestyle, Jolie was in for a shock, and must have felt like she was in bootcamp. Of her life pre-*Tomb Raider*, Jolie said, 'I smoked a lot, drank far too much, suffered from insomnia and, like every other person I know, was imbalanced. I had to undergo a complete readjustment when I started filming. From the time I got up in the morning I had to drink a certain amount of water, had protein checks with food experts, ate egg whites and took vitamins, and all the bad things in my life were taken away.' She also claimed that she'd 'never eaten so much' in her life.

Despite the fact that it was all a bit of a shock to her system, she approached her new regime with gusto and relished the change in her lifestyle. As someone who had always been naturally lithe, Jolie was instructed to gain 20lb in muscle so she could achieve a curvier physique. 'I get up at seven in the morning and do yoga, which is insane!' said Jolie. 'I'm on protein shakes, I'm doing bungee ballet, diving and weapons training with the Special Forces. I'm doing kick boxing – everything from soccer to rowing.'

According to her dad, this sporting ability was something that his daughter always had in her. 'Angie was always very athletic,' said Voight. 'When I used to coach soccer, she was the best player on the team and the best at running in her class.'

Unlike many Hollywood actresses who would rather cut off one of their arms than gain a few extra pounds, Jolie loved her physical transformation and found that it made her feel at her most attractive. In fact, if anything, the actress wished she could have gained more weight. 'I prefer curvy women but I could only get so curvy, because I am very lanky and angular. But to finally have some decent breasts and a backside is great.'

Beauty is power, as they say, and Angelina had never felt so in control of her life. 'She [Lara] made me feel beautiful for the first time in my life,' she remarked. 'We filmed much of the movie in Cambodia and I was in the best physical shape of my life. I loved running through the jungle, getting very sweaty and enjoying the fact that I was playing this very physically threatening character. Since that time I've felt confident in my looks. I wake up not thinking that I'm odd looking but that I'm beautiful.'

How she could ever have looked at her reflection and come to the conclusion that she was odd looking is almost beyond comprehension, but one thing's for certain: her husband liked the new look almost as much as she did. Lara is known for her large breasts, and Jolie's training ensured that she gained weight in that specific area. 'These babies have grown too,' said Jolie, referring to her breasts. 'Boy, am I popular at home!'

Previously a size 36C, Angelina managed to go up to a D cup for the film, but, given that Lara is a DD, Angelina had to wear a padded bra for filming. Needs must though and as Jolie herself said, 'She has to have her braid, her breasts, her boots.'

As a lover of costumes, Billy Bob was also more than happy to let Angelina dress for the part. 'I have never worn such tight clothes. No one has seen me in a tight T-shirt and little shorts in my life. My husband was more than a little confused. It was like "What are you wearing?" With the shorts, braided hair and playfulness, she is a sexy woman.'

While Jolie was undoubtedly having the time of her life making this movie, the absence of Billy Bob was at times too much for the actress to bear. And unfortunately for her, Angelina's husband had such an acute fear of flying that it was unlikely he was going to show up on set to support her too often. This meant that Angelina spent any time off jetting back to LA to see him, even if she could only stay for a few hours. 'Over those eight months I must have gone back [to LA] 30 times. I've gone back just to have him for six hours. I'm kind of an insane woman and I send him odd faxes and call him all the time and talk to him when I'm falling asleep so I feel like he's next to me.'

If all this seems a bit one-sided, Billy Bob did overcome his fear on one momentous occasion, and his bravery didn't go unnoticed by his wife. 'He doesn't fly at all,' said Jolie. 'But he managed to come to England. I called him and said, "I need you." I told him I was going to lose my mind if he didn't get over here. I need him. In my bed! He was willing to do it for me and that was an incredible moment for us because it showed me again how much he loves me.'

Billy admitted that he found it easier to board a plane if his wife was actually with him, because then the thought of dying in a crash didn't seem so daunting. 'If I'm flying with her I don't even think about it any more because I guarantee if something happened to us together we'd look each other in the eye and smile and that would be it, you know? We complete each other.'

Ever the drama queen, Angelina claimed that, if Billy Bob hadn't made the effort to get himself over to England, there was a good chance his wife was going to resort to drastic measures and admitted that at one point his not being there was affecting her performance so much that she considered sending someone over to the States to kidnap him! 'I was really no good to anyone at that point,' she admitted.

While the long-distance phone calls were a comfort to the

couple, sometimes they just made things harder. 'We'd talk at the end of the night and we'd scream with frustration down the phone. It was terrible!' And, given how physically gruelling her days on set were, Angelina found it hard to deal with her numerous injuries alone. On one particular occasion, she went to bed clutching at his clothes. 'I threw a knee out and I was badly scratched. I was really frightened. I'd go to bed hugging a pair of Billy Bob's boots or some of his T-shirts I take with me on location for comfort and go to sleep thinking, "Gimme lemon meringue pie, gimme apple pie, gimme some comfort food please!"'

In *Tomb Raider*, we see Lara swinging from the rafters of her Surrey mansion, running through jungles and fighting with her arch rivals Manfred Powell (played by Iain Glen) and Alex West (played by Daniel Craig). Although it would have been perfectly acceptable for Jolie to employ the help of a stunt double, she was reluctant to do so and, throughout filming, she insisted on giving everything a whirl herself. Her stunt co-ordinator referred to her as 'the most stubborn woman I have ever met' and West had concerns that, at times, she was putting herself at risk. 'She was totally fearless. I had to decide how much jeopardy I wanted to put her in and how much I wanted to beat her up. She was swinging on a moving log hanging 50 feet off a concrete floor and she wanted to take the safety harness off. If she fell, she would be dead. I didn't need that.'

When Jolie said that secretly she'd always 'wanted to be

Indiana Jones or James Bond', she obviously wasn't joking. In fact, when West first approached her to do the film it was the 'warrior aspect' that interested Jolie the most and within days of filming she had become 'really attached to the guns'. She said that she'd 'never thought of women as not being strong' and she was determined to prove her theory. This wasn't without its drawbacks, though, and the actress ended up injured on more than one occasion. 'I got a lot of cuts, bruises, skin burns and blisters from the harness that I wore for the stunts. After a week it got a little sore, so the stunt crew made me a fur-lined harness. It was a joke, but I'm taking it home and I'll see what Billy and I can do with it.'

And it turns out she wasn't quite as fearless as everyone presumed her to be. 'The most terrifying thing for me was definitely the bungee stuff,' admitted Jolie. 'Although I'm reliably informed that canoeing up and down the Thames was probably far more hazardous for my health.'

Like West, Jolie's dad, who had a small role in the film, was also nervous about how far she was taking things, but was the first to admit that she had inherited her determination from him. 'Like her, I want to do as much as possible myself, so I can't scold her for it. I can only say, "Take every precaution,"' said Voight. 'She's done things I couldn't do, and I wish she wouldn't.'

Despite his reservations, Voight was clearly very proud of his daughter's achievements. 'She's very handy, she's very clever, she's worked very hard and trained well, and she's very gifted in the physical arts. She's quite something as you'll see in the film, she's very strong. She certainly is an action hero, you believe her.' And he shouldn't have been surprised by his daughter's abilities, given how, even as a child, she had displayed talent in that department. 'Angie always was an athlete,' said Voight. 'When she was little, I coached a soccer team and Angie was the youngest. I put her in key situations because she was the best. I used to tell her she was an unusual athlete.'

Michael Cristofer, who had directed Angelina in *Gia* and had become a friend of the actress, had his own theories about her daredevil approach, suggesting that all her energy was coming from the fact that she'd come through all the depression she'd suffered from in the past and was in a much more positive state of mind. 'When she did *Lara Croft* she needed to find and explore and live inside that part of her personality that was strong and healthy and physically in extraordinary shape,' said Cristofer. 'I think she had come out of this really bad time and she was getting herself together in a good way through the shoot of that film.'

All the physical exertion certainly enhanced Angelina's sexual side and, much to the delight of *Tomb Raider* fans across the world, she was more than happy to let this be conveyed in her portrayal of Lara. 'I think Lara is extremely sexual,' said Jolie. 'I felt very sexual during that film. When you are ready to fight your adrenalin is going, you're on fire. It's the same feeling you get when you want to have sex.'

Again, this was a side effect of *Tomb Raider* that more than benefited her husband. 'I think Billy is excited because he knows I want him. I am very focused on him. I am hunting him down. He'll just have to brace himself because I knock him over every time I see him!'

Although the film is very much centred around action scenes, Jolie manages to make Croft flirtatious, witty and just the right side of obnoxious, and the film doesn't take itself too seriously. This was a conscious decision from the start, when she and West agreed that the tone should be 'campy and stupid'.

There was room for one scene of a more serious nature, however, and this is where Jon Voight came into play. Angelina and her father hadn't worked together since she appeared in *Lookin' to Get Out* when she was seven years old. It was something they had talked about but they came to the conclusion that it would either 'be a very good, or very bad idea.' When Angelina first read the script, the relationship between Lara and her beloved father stood out for her, and it added a more human dimension to the action girl. 'Simon and I talked about her, about her relationship with her father, and she became kind of beautiful to me,' said Jolie. She felt like she could relate to the way Lara felt about her father and decided that, if she and Voight were going to do anything together, this should be it. 'We'd waited for years before working together... as soon as I realised this was going to be such a great movie, I said it was OK to ask him.'

Above: Angelina Jolie's acting career began when she was just five years old. She is pictured here starring alongside her father Jon Voight in the 1982 movie, *Lookin' To Get Out*.

© *WENN*

As a child Angelina was definitely a Daddy's girl – she frequently attended awards ceremonies with him.

Lower left: Angelina and her father arrive at the Governor's Ball at the 58th Academy Awards Ceremony, Los Angeles 1986.

Lower right: Angelina, her father, and her brother James Haven at the 1988 Oscars Award Ceremony, Los Angeles.

© *REX Features*

When she was 16, Angelina began to appear in various music videos. She is seen here starring in the videos for Antonello Venditti's 'Alta Marea' (*above*) and The Rolling Stones's 'Anybody Seen My Baby' (*below*).

Above: A film still from *Hackers*, the first major in film in which Jolie played the lead role.

Below left: With her then husband Jonny Lee Miller, whom she met when she was just 19 on the set of *Hackers*.

Below right: In 1998 Angelina landed the lead role in the TV series *Gia*, a programme about the life of the drug-abusing supermodel Gia Marie Carangi, and finally achieved the critical acclaim that she deserved.

Above: Starring in 1996 film *Foxfire*. Once again she fell for one of her co-stars – Jenny Shimizu, a Japanese-American model turned actress.

Below: In 2000 Jolie won the Oscar for 'Best Supporting Actress' for her portrayal of Lisa Rowe alongside Winona Ryder in *Girl Interrupted*.

© WENN

Jenny Shimizu, Ange's lesbian lover.

Above: In 2000 Angelina Jolie took on her most physically demanding role to date, Lara Croft – a loud, physical woman with long dark hair, and a hot body. Jolie was a perfect match for the sexy action hero.

© *WENN*

Below left: Angelina at the Golden Globe Awards during her more vampy, Goth-like, days, 2001.

Below right: With her second husband Billy Bob Thornton at the London premiere of *Tomb Raider*. It is visible how smitten the couple were with one another.

© *REX Features*

With Colin Farrell, another co-star that she allegedly had a fling with. © *REX Features*

Playing in a park in Beverly Hills with her most precious love, her newly adopted baby son Maddox.

Lara's dad may be dead, but he is a big presence in her life and comes back to give his daughter guidance. On the anniversary of his death, Lara visits his grave and it's the only point in the film when we see the vulnerable and sentimental side to her character. Lord Richard Croft was a huge influence on Lara's life and she followed in his footsteps in terms of both career and morals. Although Voight and Jolie had a very tempestuous relationship, it was going through a more harmonious phase at the time and Jolie was more than happy to embrace the similarities between her and her character's father–daughter relationship. 'Much of this story is about her reconnecting with her father,' said Jolie. 'He's passed away, but left messages for her. She's grown up and ended up just like him. In my life my dad wasn't always there. But he always sent me letters, books, information, and in the end we did the same thing with our lives. So our scenes together ended up very personal.' So personal that they actually played with the script until they got the dialogue just right. 'We adjusted little things, maybe a word here or there, so we were really speaking to each other,' said Jolie.

She described working together as 'awesome', although, as the director, West found the whole thing quite intimidating and remarked that having Voight on set 'sometimes felt like taking a girl out on a date and have her father come along too!'

Voight was equally effusive about the whole experience.

'We just have this one scene together, but it was a wonderful thing for us to be able to work together. It was a great dream come true. We're hoping to work together many times in our lives.' He also conceded that his part wasn't too much of a stretch, given the parallels between his and Sir Richard's relationship with their daughters. 'Lara's father is trying to give her information over the years, and that's what the basic story is about. As all parents do, they try to write a little letter here and there with information, you know?'

He may have been the veteran actor on set, but it became instantly clear to Voight that his daughter was wearing the trousers in this working relationship. Opinionated as ever, his feisty Angelina was only too happy to put him in his place and he was more than happy to take her direction. While rehearsing their lines together, Voight would make suggestions, only to be told by his daughter, 'No, I'd never say or do that.' 'And she was absolutely right,' admits Voight. 'I was like a secretary; I'd write down everything she said – and that's what we'd do.' Shortly after filming was finished, Voight said that he felt the golf course was now the only place he could teach his daughter something.

While Jolie knew exactly what she wanted Lara to say, it wasn't so easy for her to learn how to say it. Surrey-born Lara was raised in an aristocratic family and perfecting the cut-glass English accent was essential for Jolie. She had several sessions with a dialect coach and the end result is pretty impressive, despite the fact that at times she found it hard not to 'slip into cockney'. Another area that needed work, or rather needed concealing, was Angelina's tattoos. Given that she has several and Lara Croft has none, the make-up artists on set had their work cut out trying to cover them all up. At first, the actress was keen to show them off but then decided that she would rather Lara was not identical to her and, besides, she knew it was unlikely that an English aristocrat would have the name Billy Bob inked on to her arm! After leaving Gordonstoun school, Lara attended a Swiss finishing school and, in accordance with this, Jolie was sent to, as she called it, 'manners school'. Lara may be a fighter, but everything she does, she does with grace and good posture, and this was something else that the somewhat gangly Angelina had to get a handle on.

Perhaps the most overwhelming element of the whole *Tomb Raider* experience for Jolie, above and beyond all the training and elocution lessons, was the fact that she hadn't quite anticipated what a big deal it was to play Lara Croft. 'I didn't realise what I'd gotten myself into. She's such an icon and a male fantasy figure,' she admitted. 'I thought I would do a movie, learn a lot and enjoy the experience. There is massive expectation. A lot of people play the *Tomb Raider* game series and have their views on what Lara should or should not be like. I hope I live up to expectations.' There was one area she was confident in, however, and that was her appearance. 'I was worried about disappointing people, but at least no one is complaining about me looking the part!'

Jolie hadn't banked on the sense of ownership that die-hard *Tomb Raider* fans felt towards Lara and, while she was happy to do interviews and promote the film, she was a tad freaked out by the fact that there would soon be replica dolls all over the world and people would essentially be able to have her in their house. When she was confronted with the Lara Croft merchandise, Jolie was slightly disturbed. 'Seeing yourself in plastic is just one of the most bizarre things that can happen to you. I can just imagine someone taking the head off and setting it on fire or sticking me upside down in mud.' She felt compromised and admitted that the first time she saw herself as a doll she had to try 'really hard not to cry' and thought, 'Why has someone superimposed a gun right in between my legs? I don't like seeing her in that position!'

She also battled to take the size of the Lara doll's breasts 'down a notch' after the makers had given her something of an enhancement in that area. All of this was probably much easier for Billy Bob to deal with, given that he was married to one of the most lusted-after women in the world, and of the film's promotion he proudly stated that his wife was 'going to be on every McDonald's cup in the world'! It was exactly that level of fame that Angelina was so scared of, though. While *Girl, Interrupted* had won her an Oscar, it certainly didn't attract the level of attention that *Tomb Raider* did, and Jolie wasn't prepared to be a world-famous celebrity, claiming that 'it could fuck with your head... It could be the thing that sends me... back into the mental institution.'

She had no need to worry, though, for, although Angelina had made it clear how nervous she was about the film's reception, cinema-goers whooped and cheered at early screenings of the film and the actress couldn't have been more relieved. 'That's the greatest thing,' she said. 'Hopefully they know I'm a friend. And I'm very, very human, and very flawed. I'm not separated from them, I'm one of them.'

This may have been the case, but it's much more likely that the cheering had something to do with the fact that she was running around looking gorgeous in a very tight T-shirt and hotpants...

chapter 9

angelina the humanitarian

When Angelina returned to Billy Bob and LA after filming *Tomb Raider*, it wasn't just her appearance that had changed. Being away from home for so long had exposed her to new cultures, different perspectives and a much broader view of the world, and, much to his dismay, Thornton found that Jolie was now a very different woman to the one he married. One of the main things that influenced this change was the fact that Jolie spent much of her time in England watching the news, and she was amazed by what an eye opener this was for her. Having grown up in America, she felt like she'd only ever heard one version of events, whatever the story, and being in the UK opened her eyes to a lot of things she had never been exposed to before. 'Growing up in the States, I learned about American history and that was the extent of it. I focused on what was affecting us, not the rest of the world,' said Jolie. 'After watching the news in England I realised just how sheltered from the world we are in the States.'

Another part of the *Tomb Raider* experience that had affected Angelina in a big way was the time she spent filming in Cambodia, a place which she would go on to describe as 'the most beautiful place I've ever been'. The actress was overwhelmed, not only by the beauty of the country, but also by the kindness of the people, and she couldn't quite believe that a large number of Cambodians were still suffering from the effects of the civil war.

Since the 1970s, there had been long periods of fighting between different factions vying for power in the country and Cambodia's troubled history left many problems for its people. In 1975, the Khmer Rouge regime took control and under their leadership an estimated two million Cambodians – around a quarter of the population – died through starvation, deaths in refugee camps, disease, forced labour or being tortured or murdered by the government. Between 1978 and 1989, there was a war between the Khmer Rouge and the neighbouring country of Vietnam. A peace declaration was signed in 1991, but years of turmoil had destroyed the social, cultural, economic and political life of Cambodia. Another legacy of the long years of war are the millions of unexploded landmines that are still in place. Forty thousand Cambodians have suffered amputations as a result of mine injuries since 1979.

After visiting the country, Jolie described the people as 'so generous and open, kind and spiritual' and said that, prior to her visit, she'd had 'no idea that kids are still stepping on land mines every day. It was really eye opening for me.'

Angelina was hugely sympathetic to the dire situation the people of Cambodia found themselves in, and she knew that she had to act on her feelings as soon as she returned to the States. Unclear as to what exactly she could do to help, Jolie contacted the United Nations High Commission for Refugees (UNHCR) and said that if there was anything she could do she would. And, wisely, Jolie knew that her movie-star status would inevitably help her reach out to people and get them to listen in a way that an unknown would struggle to do. 'If I can use this celebrity thing in a positive way, that might mean young people get involved, it has to be worth it,' she explained. Angelina was also honest about the fact that her yearning to learn about countries less fortunate than her own was not entirely a selfless act. 'Selfishly, I knew it would change my life to really understand,' admitted Jolie. It's unlikely that the actress knew at this stage the extent to which it would change her life.

Soon after getting in touch with the UNHCR, Angelina set off on the first of many UN trips to Sierra Leone and Tanzania in July 2001 on an educational tour and on the way home she had something of an epiphany. 'I had gone from being in the African jungle to sitting on a first-class flight home,' recalled Jolie. 'Though I was covered in dirt, I felt real and at my most beautiful. And suddenly, I was surrounded by people who knew me as an actress. I think my appearance was upsetting to all of them, in their suits and make-up, looking at magazines. I felt sick because I started flipping through the articles about parties, film ratings, who has this, who's the hottest that. I felt like I didn't want to return to that world.'

Angelina had never been one to embrace the more glamorous side of fame. While she could don a designer dress like the best of them and look a million dollars, scoring points on the best-dressed lists was certainly never one of her ambitions. To her, acting wasn't something that she did to achieve an A-list lifestyle. On the contrary, the luxuries it afforded her were something she could take or leave.

However strongly she felt about the plight of these poverty-stricken countries, Angelina was wary of airing her views publicly for fear of looking like a flippant and whimsical celeb who had jumped on a bandwagon. She was also more than aware of the fact that her rather vampiric reputation preceded her and that she might not be taken seriously in a political arena. 'It's very upsetting for me,' admitted Jolie. 'People always think I'm crazy and a bit weird, so I'm very careful about my politics because I don't want things to get caught up in the silliness of what is written about me. But I do feel very strongly that we need better news here in LA. We don't pay close attention to the world.'

When it came to being taken seriously, Jolie had her work cut out at home as much as she did anywhere else in the world. While he was initially supportive of his wife's newfound passion, Billy Bob was more than a little sceptical about what exactly she was hoping to achieve by visiting these countries. According to Jolie, 'He would say "Why are you going to do these things? What do you think you're going to accomplish?" It seems crazy to some of my friends that I want to leave the warmth and safety of my home. But I had to believe I could accomplish something.'

Her family and friends were equally sceptical and didn't understand why Angelina had to visit these countries in person. If she was keen to help, why couldn't she just help from a distance? Angelina's answer was simple. 'I don't understand exactly what's going on unless I am inside a place,' she revealed.

When it came to leaving for Sierra Leone, her tearful mother gave her a message from her brother, saying, 'Tell Angie I love her and to remember that, if she is ever scared, sad or angry, look up at the night sky, find the second star on the right, and follow it straight on till morning.' This was a reference to *Peter Pan*, which had been one of their favourite stories when they were growing up.

Marcheline's fears for her daughter's safety weren't helped by the fact that she had to write a cheque for insurance to cover Angelina in case she was kidnapped or had to be airlifted out of somewhere. Equally concerned, Jon Voight actually took it upon himself to call the UNHCR and begged them to cancel his daughter's planned trip. Given that Angelina was an adult, and therefore old enough to make her own decisions, his pleas got him nowhere, but this didn't stop her from being annoyed with her dad. 'I was angry with him,' she said, 'but I told him that I know he loves me and that as my father he was trying to protect me from harm.'

Unperturbed by her family's protestations, Jolie spent a large part of 2001 on UNHCR missions, visiting Africa, Cambodia and Pakistan, and then Ecuador in 2002. This may have separated her from her husband for weeks at a time, but Jolie had been bitten by the humanitarian bug and, as far as she was concerned, there was no going back. She decided to write a diary while on these missions and her memoirs, *Notes from My Travels*, were published in October 2003, with all proceeds going to the UNHCR.

Jolie's book is a moving and enlightening read, and she writes about her experiences simply and without pretension. When she started to work for the UNHCR, she was the first to admit her ignorance about the plight of refugees and it's clear that she didn't go on these trips to play the role of the big movie star doing a good turn, but to listen, to look and to learn. 'I do not know what I will accomplish,' she said. 'All I do know is that while I was learning more and more every day about the world... I realised how much I didn't know.'

Rather than bombard the reader with political facts and

self-righteous sermons, she describes the situations she saw, how they made her feel and what could be done to help in an honest and straightforward fashion. As you would expect, she was often confronted with horrendous situations, the like of which she'd never seen before, and she takes us through every emotion she felt, every tear she shed and every person who touched her in some way. She lists the shocking statistics that propelled her into action: more than 20 million refugees exist today; one-sixth of the world's population lives on less than one dollar a day; 1.1 billion people lack access to safe drinking water; one-third of the world has no electricity; more than 100 million children are out of school; one in six children in Africa dies before the age of five. She also talks about how the education she received from her work had 'forever changed' her. 'I am so grateful I took this path in my life,' she wrote. 'Thankful that I met these amazing people and had this incredible experience.'

She visited Africa from 22 February to 9 March and was hugely affected by the sights of deprivation that she saw first hand. She also became self-conscious about her occupation and at first wanted to conceal from people that she was an actress for fear that her chosen career would appear futile and shallow. 'What I do is a strange job for them to imagine,' said Jolie, but she soon realised that these people had no conception of her fame and fortune and were unfazed by the fact that she was an actress. If they looked excited to see her, it was to do with the fact that she had arrived in a UN truck, not because she had won an Oscar. So much so, in fact, that one little girl asked for the Hollywood star's address. At first Jolie was reluctant to hand out such private details. 'I thought for a moment about maintaining my privacy, as I have been told to do in the States,' she said. 'But they shared with me, so I'll share with them.' The refugees didn't care about who she was, or what films she made, they just cared that she was there and she was trying to help.

Also conscious of her wealth, Jolie found that she wanted to rid herself of any jewellery or items of clothing that may have appeared showy. 'I did not want to flash anything of value,' she said, 'not because I feared theft, but because I felt bad. I walked around people who were living with so little.' This was a whole new world for the privileged Jolie and, although she wasn't always sure how to act in certain situations, she was adamant that she wouldn't offend anyone. On one occasion, she took the hand of a child, knowing that the child might have had scabies. While most people would shy away from physical contact in such a situation, Jolie was keen to prove that she wasn't precious. 'I would rather get infected than to ever think about pulling my hands away from these little children,' she said. When asked if she'd ever give up acting and dedicate her life to charity work, Jolie said, 'I would love to, but I know I am more useful as an actress. If I do a film, I am able financially to do a lot of good and bring more attention [than] if I only spend a week in a field. That's how I am more useful. I could build a school with my bare hands over a year, or I could buy hundreds of schools. I'm just aware that I can do more with my foot in this door.'

She became so attached to the people that she met in Africa that she wanted to keep all memories of them close to her, even if it meant forgoing hygiene! On her flight from Dar es Salaam to London, Jolie found that she was reluctant to remove the filthy jacket she had been wearing throughout her trip, and admitted, 'It has been my blanket. I don't want to clean up or wash off this place. For some reason, taking off my jacket, I feel I am detaching myself from all the people – the places...'

In spite of herself, however, it wasn't long before Jolie had settled back into her luxurious LA lifestyle. 'I was embarrassed to realise [and to admit] how [easily] I was able to return to my life after Africa,' she confessed.

It was therefore very important for the actress to plan a second trip, this time to Cambodia. Having fallen in love with the country after shooting scenes for the first *Tomb Raider* there, her second visit – which took place between 16 and 27 July – confirmed it in her own mind as the country from which she would choose a child for adoption. Highlights of her trip to her future son Maddox's homeland included detonating a landmine with the chemical explosive TNT. 'It was a great feeling to destroy something that would have otherwise hurt or killed another person,' she admitted. She also got to meet Luong Ung, the author of her favourite book, *First They Killed My Father*, which was a great honour for the actress. Angelina had been greatly affected by Ung's personal account of her experiences during the Khmer Rouge years and was greatly in awe of her. In her book, Ung, whose father was a wealthy government worker and a target for the Khmer Rouge, describes how her entire family had to flee their home and pretend to be a farming family in an attempt to escape being murdered. Ung was five years old at the start of the Pol Pot regime and grew up living in fear and surrounded by uncertainty. After being trained as a female soldier, she eventually escaped to Vietnam and made her way to America, but not before one of her sisters and her beloved father were murdered.

This young woman's experiences humbled Jolie and she admits that she felt 'nervous' when she came face to face with her heroine. There was no need to feel worried, though. The two women made an instant connection and Ung was very grateful to Jolie for raising awareness of the problems in Cambodia. 'It only took moments for our eyes to meet,' recalls Jolie. 'We smiled as we walked up to one another, and we hugged as if we had known each other for years.' In one highly personal anecdote in her journals, Angelina describes an evening with Ung during which, just after putting up their hammocks one night, they set out with a flashlight to find a spot to relieve themselves. 'I held the flashlight. She had two handfuls of toilet paper. We both found spots just off the road about ten feet apart.'

Jolie also talks of how difficult she found it to cope with her contact lenses in the Cambodian rain and, in an almost childlike manner, describes how she thinks she'd cope if she lived there permanently. 'It was hard for me to see with so much water in my eyes,' said the actress. 'I think about the fact that if I lived here I wouldn't have the luxury of contacts, and in this weather, with my glasses on, I wouldn't be able to see a thing.'

Another aspect of Cambodian life she struggled with was the water shortage; Jolie was so conscious of not wasting any that she preferred to stay dirty. 'I still can't manage to pour the water over myself right,' she said. 'And I don't want to waste the water.'

The next stop for Jolie was Pakistan and, in August of the same year, she spent a week meeting refugees and learning from the UNHCR representatives there. Ironically, she often felt more comfortable with the people of Pakistan than she did with representatives from the UNHCR and the American Embassy, and admitted that she was often intimidated by their knowledge of world affairs. 'Sometimes I get scared when everyone else talks politics,' she said. 'But... what I learned was that the observations and feelings of an individual who is trying to understand are just as important.'

Jolie has visited Washington DC over 20 times and met with congressmen and senators to lobby humanitarian efforts and admits that, again, it is a situation she is intimidated by. 'I put my head together, cover my tattoos, get into my suits, look clean, don't dress sexy and try to present the woman I'm not sure I am but would like to aspire to be a little more,' admitted Jolie. Although in theory she had less in common with the refugees than she did with the political figures she was meeting, she found that she was much more at home with them, particularly the women. 'We shared opinions, laughter, loving our husbands and wanting a future for our children,' said the actress warmly.

Just two weeks after returning from this trip, the events of 9/11 shocked the world and Angelina's continued public support of the people of the Middle East sparked some controversy in the US. She went on Larry King's show on CNN and talked openly about how not all Afghans should be punished for the horrendous events, commenting, 'I think for many people it's not a very popular thing to talk about. But they are families just like our families and they are a beautiful people and a tortured people.'

In *Notes from My Travels*, she describes the threats she received after appearing on the show. 'Not forgetting the Afghan families I had met just weeks before, I spoke out about their need for relief and I personally made a donation. In the days that followed, I received three death threats, including a phone call,' said Jolie. 'The man told me he thought all Afghans should suffer for what they did in New York City and that he wished for everyone in my family to die.' Nearly 3,000 people had died at the hands of Islamic extremists when the Twin Towers were destroyed, so Jolie wasn't surprised that her opinions had caused upset. 'Emotions were running high,' she said. 'I understand that. It was a difficult time for everyone.'

The death threats may have scared Angelina, but they certainly didn't put her off continuing her work as a humanitarian, and eight months later she made a trip to Ecuador to take a look at what she described as the 'Western Hemisphere's most severe humanitarian crisis', with Colombia having one of the worst internal displacement problems in the world. This trip was a little bit different for Jolie in the sense that it was the first one since she had become a mother and, while she was still incredibly dedicated to her work for the UNHCR, she found it hard to leave her new son behind. 'It was ridiculous how emotional I felt kissing him goodbye,' she admitted. Becoming a mother and experiencing the feelings of protectiveness that people naturally feel towards their children also served to increase her already huge admiration for the people who dedicated their lives to aid work. 'I can't imagine how the UNHCR staff does it when they are posted in a no-family duty station,' she confessed. 'They go months without seeing their children. You ask them about it and they will tell you how hard it is. Everyone has pictures, but then they say the people they work with – the refugees – many have lost their children. So they at least know their families are safe.'

As difficult as Jolie may have found it to tear herself away from her baby, her efforts were not in vain and, in August 2001, she was made a Goodwill Ambassador for the UN.

Rudd Lubbers, the UN High Commissioner for Refugees, had nothing but good things to say about Jolie's contributions to the UNHCR. In the foreword to her book, he wrote, 'Our challenges are immense, and they could not be met without the dedicated support of concerned individuals around the world. One such champion of the refugee cause is Angelina Jolie. Since her appointment [as Goodwill Ambassador], Angelina has more than fulfilled my expectations. She has proven to be a close partner and a genuine colleague in our efforts to find solutions for the world's refugees. Her personal generosity and her truly compassionate spirit are an inspiration to us all.'

Shannon Boyd, who also worked for the UNHCR, said that, when Jolie visited dangerous countries, she never once heard the actress ask if she was going to be safe there, or make any diva-like demands. 'She has never complained about conditions, even though at times they have been very arduous indeed,' said Boyd. 'She has a very easy rapport with all the refugees she meets. They sense she will go away and do something to help them. She gives them hope. Children have been named after her in refugee camps all over the world.'

Another spokesperson for the charity, Joung-Ah Ghedini, also had nothing but admiration for Jolie's attitude, saying, 'If it means riding a rickety motorcycle for six hours into regions where she can't even have a shower, she will.'

Apart from her Goodwill Ambassador accolade, Jolie has also gone on to be the first recipient of the Citizen of the World Award from the United Nations Correspondents Association in 2003 and the Global Humanitarian Award from the UNA-USA in 2005. In 2005, Jolie was also awarded Cambodian citizenship for the conservation work she has done there.

Angelina's trip to Ecuador in June 2002 is the fourth and final trip that she documents in her memoirs and, at the end of the book, she talks about the factors that ensure her commitment to her charity work. 'The beginning of the United Nations charter is "We the peoples",' she wrote. 'It's one of the most beautiful things I have ever read – and that's what it is; the life spent together, all the people of the world, protecting our history, our cultures and learning from each other. Refugees are families and individuals just like us but they don't have the freedom we have. Their human rights have been violated.'

To this day, Angelina, who once said that she'd like to die knowing she'd been useful, continues to campaign for human rights across the globe and has donated millions of dollars over the years to a variety of causes that are important to her, including the refugees of Afghanistan who fled the Taliban, poverty-stricken farmers in Cambodia, AIDS clinics in Ethiopia, victims of a prolonged conflict in the western Sahara, and the Millennium Project, which aims to halve world poverty by 2015. 'It's ridiculous to think that you earn that in a year and you should just keep it because you need three cars and you need two houses – that's stupid,' said Jolie, who has donated a third of her income to charity since 2001. 'I think you should give away as much as possible.'

Apart from financial contributions, Jolie, who was subsequently named one of the 25 most influential philanthropists in the world in the business publication *Worth*, continues to be committed to raising awareness of several issues, which requires a lot more than just putting pen to paper and writing a cheque. She has started two foundations – the Maddox Relief Project, which deals with Cambodia, and the Jolie Foundation, which helps children in orphanages. And, in 2005, she made three documentaries, two for MTV, one of which was entitled *The Diary of Angelina Jolie and Dr Jeffrey D Sachs*. Sachs was the deputy of the United Nations Secretary General, Kofi Annan, and the man behind the Millennium Project. In the documentary, we follow Sachs and Jolie on their trip to the Kenyan village of Sauri and see them meeting the locals and witnessing the effects of malnutrition, lack of clean water and poor health care. Jolie also presented another documentary, *Inhuman Traffic*, also made for MTV, which focused on Europe's sex-trafficking trade. Jolie hoped the programme would 'empower women and girls', saying, 'It is a tragedy that in the 21st century hundreds of thousands of people are trafficked and exploited every year.'

The next documentary Jolie made was *A Moment In The*

World, which captured events as they occurred all over the world during the same random three-minute time frame. This idea stemmed from the fact that one day Jolie could be in Cambodia, where people live in fear of stepping on a landmine, and then within 24 hours she'd be back to living in the lap of luxury in LA. 'I kept going between Mad's country and refugee camps or war zones to Hollywood and all these odd places and then seeing the world at all these different times,' said Jolie. She saw the film as a great way to show those who led more privileged lives just how deprived life can be elsewhere. 'You don't have to live with nothing to be a good person,' said Jolie. 'But, once you've seen people suffering, how can you not remember it all the time and do something towards making things better? How can you not do something? It sounds corny but I want to make things better in the world, so whatever it takes to do that, I'm there.'

chapter 10

the break-up

Although Jolie had been consumed with her charity work in 2001, there was something else playing on her mind at this time, and she knew that the time was right to make a big change in her life. For Angelina, the time was right to become a mother. Although the actress had always expressed a desire to adopt children, she insisted on an 18-month break between filming *Lara Croft: Tomb Raider* and the sequel, *Lara Croft Tomb Raider: The Cradle of Life* so that she 'could do other things, or get pregnant'. However, when this break came, the idea of having her own child had gone to the back of Angelina's mind and now, more than ever, she was intent on adoption. And, if her husband Billy Bob was having doubts about going through with it, he must have kept his reservations to himself, for the couple started filling out adoption forms

147

together at the Immigration and Naturalization Service in LA in September 2001.

While the couple were going through the long adoption process and being interviewed by the appropriate authorities, Angelina was determined to make a contribution to the children of Cambodia, as the idea of helping only one child wasn't going to fulfil her charitable urges. 'Before I adopted Maddox, I decided to do something financially to help the whole orphanage. I can't bring every kid home, but I can make sure that life is better for a big group of them. I helped to sponsor the kids that were older, who were not going to be adopted. The first time I saw a young boy who was dying I said, "I'm going to save everybody and I'm going to solve it, let's get him airlifted out." But he was only one of 20,000 kids in that area. It's so sad.'

Despite the fact that Angelina and Billy Bob were still together, cracks were already beginning to appear in what had once been an obsessively close relationship and the couple who used to balk at the idea of leaving each other's side were now happily pursuing different interests. Billy remained devoted to his band and spent hours in the studio working on songs; in the meantime, his wife would be educating herself elsewhere on world issues. Looking back on when things started to go wrong, Angelina recalled the time when their individual pursuits started to drive a wedge between them. 'He was focusing on his music and I was upstairs reading. I went through a change in my life and started becoming more politically active. I was saying, "OK, well, you're going to finish this song and I'm going to Washington and I'll see you Monday." And then two weeks later it would be, like, "OK, I'm going to Sierra Leone and Tanzania…"'

Considering that after *Tomb Raider* Billy Bob had talked of a pact they'd made which would ensure they'd be together at all times, these voluntary separations were not a good sign. 'When she's doing a movie, I'll be with her,' Thornton had said, 'and when I'm doing one she'll be with me. We're just going to make sure that we stick pretty close together from now on because life is pretty precious these days.'

Another problem in the relationship was the fact that Thornton was reluctant to accompany his wife on her trips to refugee camps. While this may well have been down to his deep fear of flying, it was clear that the actor was also starting to resent the time and energy his wife was spending abroad. His absence from these trips cut to Angelina's heart and she found it hard to forgive him for his lack of support. 'He's never been to a refugee camp,' she said. 'I asked him to come but he chose not to. You learn what a person is about by their behaviour. And sometimes what they do hurts you.' As much as she might have blamed him, Jolie was all too aware that, while he was essentially still the same man she had married, she had changed. 'I opened myself up to wanting to learn more about the world, about other people and the things that are really going on. And so I changed.'

He may not have accompanied her on her UN missions, but Thornton was by his wife's side when it came to choosing Maddox (who was born Rath Vibol on 5 August 2001). It was in November 2001 that she and Billy made that all-important trip to Cambodia. 'Once I was approved as an adoptive parent, I decided to visit only one orphanage and leave it to destiny,' recalls Jolie. 'I was told if you want to adopt an orphan you should have a connection to the country they come from, because that's the history you're going to share with them. When I went to Cambodia with the UN, I loved the country, the people. So I went to an orphanage and there were about 15 kids in there but Maddox was the last baby I met. He was asleep but they put him in my arms and when he finally woke up we were staring at each other and I was crying and he smiled and that was it. He was three months old and they were waiting on the results of AIDS and hepatitis tests. Fortunately, he ended up being healthy, but he'd have been my son either way.'

Jolie, who had spent most of her life feeling like an outsider, found that all her worst fears banished when she met this child. She admitted that she always wondered how good she'd be as a mother, revealing, 'My discomfort with children was because I always assumed I could never make them happy because I was accused of being dark.'

Maddox was too young to accuse her of anything, though, and this level of acceptance and unconditional love was enough to make Jolie feel complete. Of all the roles this actress could take on, her most important one would be that of a mother. From this moment, she never looked back. She had finally found what she was meant to be doing in life – nurturing. And, according to her mother, it was something that she was always meant to do. 'My mother says I was talking about [adoption] since I was little.' Her childhood dream had finally come true.

Sadly, as the chapter of motherhood opened, the Billy Bob chapter was drawing to a close and, as much as it pained her to accept it, it gradually became clear that Angelina was going to be raising Maddox alone. When the final stages of adoption had gone through and the authorities finally allowed Maddox to join his new mother on 8 May, Jolie was working in Africa on *Beyond Borders* with Clive Owen, and so Maddox joined her there. The last time Billy Bob and Angelina were together properly was in March of that year, when they rented a house in Montreal while Billy was filming *Levity*.

For the majority of April and May, Billy Bob had been on tour with his beloved band, The House of Blues, and, when he returned to LA in June, it wasn't long before he set off on the road once more – and this was the point of no return in their marriage. The couple would see each other as man and wife for the last time on 3 June and, when Thornton returned to LA in July, he checked into the Sunset Marquis hotel, knowing that he was unlikely to be welcomed back into the family home with open arms.

Just as keen to avoid their troubled relationship, Angelina had herself taken refuge in a quiet establishment in the beach town of Santa Monica in order to distance herself from the memories their house in LA would provoke. Talking about the incident that finally ended their marriage, Jolie said, 'The last straw was when he took off to go on tour with his band rather than spend time with me and Maddox. I lost all my respect for him and saw that he just wasn't the kind of man I needed or wanted to be with. His behaviour was just unacceptable to me and really put things in proper perspective. I began to realise he wasn't willing to take the responsibility of helping me raise Maddox. I was disappointed and disillusioned. He turned out to be less of a man than I expected.'

And if Thornton's lack of interest in their new son wasn't enough to push her away, the rumours of his infidelity certainly were. While he was on tour, it's thought that Billy Bob wasn't exactly behaving like the devoted married man he had once been, and witnesses said that it was not unusual for him to invite girls up on stage with him and then take groupies for late-night drinking sessions after his gigs. Angelina had joked in the past that if Billy was ever unfaithful to her she wouldn't kill him because she loved his children and wanted them to have a dad, but that she wouldn't hesitate to beat him up because she knew where all his sport injuries were! Although she didn't go so far as assaulting him, Angelina did remark, 'I don't think they are untrue,' and she certainly wasn't going to put up with that kind of behaviour from someone she had once trusted with her life. 'Things had been building up, or should I say falling apart, between us for several months,' she admitted. 'He wasn't respectful of me and it was clear things were going on behind my back that I couldn't live with. I'm pretty open and tolerant, but I couldn't live with someone I no longer trusted.'

Ever the survivor, Jolie refused to let Billy Bob's behaviour keep her down and was determined that she would bring Maddox up as well as she could, with or without his support. While she admitted that she 'didn't plan on being a single parent', she was adamant that it was better not to have Thornton around if his presence wasn't going to be a positive one. 'I was pretty angry and disappointed for a time but there was nothing I could do but move on,' she said of the split. 'I found a lot of inner strength and resolve which I didn't know I had in me. It was a huge turning point in my world. It was a major evolution in my life.'

Given that her father left when Angelina was only a baby, she was only too familiar with men who were unable to cope with responsibility. Billy Bob had led her to believe that he was her partner for life, no matter what, and his failure to be there made her more determined than ever that he had no right to the title of father when it came to Maddox.

'Family is earned,' said Jolie. 'You can't just have a child, go away and then claim him or her as your child. I don't mourn the loss of my father, but I do feel sad about all the years my mom felt the need to keep us together as a family. During a divorce, some people feel they should pretend to be a happy family for Christmas or birthdays. That's a mistake, because you shouldn't have to be around somebody who makes you feel uncomfortable. I've learned from my parents' mistakes and that's why I want Maddox to be around people who are there because they want to be and not because anybody's made them.'

If she hadn't had Maddox, it's likely that the marriage break-up would have sent Jolie into a spiral of depression that she was all too familiar with, but, as it was, she was now responsible for someone else's feelings as well as her own and there was no way she was going to let him be affected by what was going on. 'I can't get into a fight or be angry because I look over and there's this kid with this silly little face. He gets sad when I'm sad. I really want to stay in a good space for him. I'm a lot stronger and more secure than anyone gives me credit for. It's true I may have gone through difficult times, but the sky doesn't fall down because another person is no longer part of your life. You take responsibility for your life and stop feeling sorry for yourself.'

Angelina wasn't without the support of her beloved mother and brother James and credits them with keeping her strong at this time. 'I am surrounded by good people, my mother, my brother, the people I work with. I've always been very close to my mother, who raised me. She's a wonderful,

wonderful woman and loving being a grandmother. I don't have a big circle of friends so she and I are very important to each other.'

She was also remarkably confident that Maddox would receive the best upbringing possible and knew that she could offer him a lot of things other kids would never dream of. 'Maddox is going to be a fortunate kid – he's going to have a great education and he's going to travel the world. He may not have a traditional father but there are many wonderful men in my life who love Maddox. He'll have male influences. It's better to have nobody than somebody who is half there, or doesn't want to be there, or is there and then disappears.'

Jolie impressed not only herself with how well she was coping alone, but also those who were close to her. Having declared to the world how her entire happiness depended on the love she and Billy Bob shared, her friends and family understandably expected the actress to struggle. 'Everyone was wondering if I would fall apart,' said Jolie. 'I guess I fooled a lot of people and showed that I'm a lot more together and self-assured than I might have been given credit for. I surprised myself.'

And, while many people in her position would have felt stupid for publicly declaring undying love for someone only to find that the relationship would crumble at the first hurdle, Jolie remained philosophical about her relationship with Thornton, saying, 'It seemed like we were passionately in love. And we were very much in love but it was a great, wonderful crush that came from fun and friendship. Then we started to do different things with our life and halfway through our marriage we became very different people and we had nothing to talk about any more and nothing in common. So it ended.' She also described their love as 'the sort of love you have in high school – it seemed obsessive but really it was just fun'.

For the first time in her life, Angelina hadn't been the one to walk away from her relationship and, also for the first time in her life, someone had completely and utterly broken her heart. As always, she was disarmingly honest about this in interviews. Unlike many Hollywood stars who gloss over break-ups with antiseptic lines such as 'work commitments drove us apart', Angelina, who had never allowed a publicist to control her public image, was much more honest than most and exposed her vulnerability to the world. 'It was as if I had this enormous trust and feeling of security in one person, and then it all vanished,' she confessed. 'I was always very open with my feelings, and I had spoken so many times in interviews about how devoted I was to this man. But, in the end, he wasn't devoted to me.'

And while the actress certainly regretted the way things had turned out between them, she certainly didn't regret anything she had ever said about him. 'I don't want, ever in my life, to be somebody who thinks about what they say and censors it. I believe that, if you're going to do an interview, you might as well share something that means something to someone who reads it. We're all here to communicate with each other. Maybe the mistakes I've made, and how I've recovered from them, might help somebody. Nobody identifies with a perfect person.'

In the aftermath of their break-up, Billy Bob was equally candid about his regrets, admitting, 'I walked away. It's the most stupid thing I've ever done. I fell in love – the hardest I've ever fallen – and it was a scary thing. Nothing was her fault, absolutely nothing. It was all down to me.' He also conceded that he had been 'selfish' and, according to Danielle Dotzenrod, the model he dated after the split, it was clear that he was 'still in love with Angelina'. Given that he had once said, 'A day can only be so bad when you wake up with Angelina by your side,' it came as no surprise to anyone that he would feel remorseful about what had happened.

Angelina said that, when she brought Maddox home, Billy 'behaved like a baby himself' and it's clear that her husband couldn't cope without his wife's undivided attention. The actor had admitted to feelings of inadequacy in the past, saying, 'I'm not an ultra-confident type of guy. I'm insecure and often feel out of place,' and clearly he just wasn't strong enough to share Angelina with Maddox. While she was typically effusive about her feelings for Maddox, all Billy Bob had to say about his new son was that, 'His hair stands straight up, like he was born a punk rocker.' Compared to his wife's outpourings of love this seemed a bit detached, and it was clear that Billy may have seen Maddox as a threat as opposed to embracing the new addition to their family. One thing Billy was adamant about was the fact that he wasn't unfaithful during the marriage. 'I didn't cheat,' he insisted. 'But it was my fault. It was my feelings of inadequacy and fear. I was frightened of Angie because she was too good for me. She was too beautiful and too smart. She was my best friend and the love of my life.'

Rumour has it that, after their separation, Billy Bob bombarded Angelina with calls and letters begging her to take him back, but as far as the actress was concerned Billy had had his chance and he'd blown it. After her split with Jonny Lee Miller, Angelina had nothing but praise for the actor and blamed herself for the breakdown in their relationship, but with Billy it was a different story entirely. Clearly bitter about her ex, Jolie said, 'I feel like I don't know him at all. We don't talk. We're not friends. I don't actually know if we'd want to see each other again. We were not meant to be together and we're better off without each other.'

Jolie admitted that she had moved out of their house when Billy was away so as not to bump into him and she had seen fit to remove the 'Till The End Of Time' artwork from above their bed. Rather than destroying it, Angelina decided to hide it in the fireplace. 'It was a lie to have it up. It was the only out of sight place in the bedroom, without being dramatic and smashing it. I don't know if he knows it's in the fireplace. I don't know if he lit a fire!' In another interview a year after the split, she was asked how she'd like to be remembered and Jolie said, 'I suppose I'm glad I'm not going to be remembered as Billy's wife. That's a good thing. That wouldn't have been the correct me if I'd died a year ago.' This was quite the opposite of what Angelina had to say after she split up with Jonny, when she maintained that she was 'very proud to have been his wife'.

Both Thornton and Jolie also went to great lengths to have the tattoos of each other's name removed from their bodies. While Billy Bob had 'Angelina' shortened to 'Angel' and had the space filled with a picture of an angel, Angelina embarked on a series of laser sessions to have 'Billy Bob' removed from her left arm. Although the actress admitted it was painful, she said she was more than 'happy to do it', and afterwards said, 'I'll never get a man's name tattooed on my body again.'

When it came to filing for a divorce, Jolie unsurprisingly applied for sole custody of Maddox (as well as stating that she wanted to keep all her earnings since the day that she and Thornton separated). Given what she perceived as his lack of interest in their son, there were no concerns on her side that Billy Bob would contest this.

While Angelina undoubtedly mourned the loss of the love of her life, Maddox introduced her to a different kind of relationship, and one that had no chance of fizzling out after a couple of years. Her son was here to stay, and nothing could have made the actress happier or more fulfilled. 'I'm beginning to accept I'm terrible at marriage,' she admitted after the divorce. But Billy Bob certainly wasn't going to put her off relationships forever. 'I'm not letting it spoil things for me,' she said. 'I have a lot of love to give.'

chapter 11

mad about the boy

A friend of Angelina's once told her that there are two types of women in life: wives and mothers and aunts and lovers. Jolie recoiled in horror when she heard this theory, convinced that she'd only ever fall into the latter category. 'I was like, "Oh no, that's me,"' she admitted. And, for a while, she was right. With her hedonistic lifestyle, temperamental relationships and penchant for the darker things in life, Angelina wasn't exactly perfect mother material. And even the actress couldn't have imagined that, a few life-changing experiences down the line, she would have transformed herself so beyond recognition. 'I'd never held a child before. When I was growing up I never babysat; I was too punk rock to be trusted,' she confessed. 'I was nervous. I knew I could love a kid, but would a child be comfortable with me – or scream and want to be in somebody else's arms?'

As we've already discovered, the shift in Jolie's priorities started to take place when she spent time in England and Cambodia filming *Tomb Raider*, where she been exposed to a side of life that she had previously been oblivious to. And so when it came to making *Beyond Borders* with Clive Owen – the story of an overprivileged American, Sarah Jordan, whose head is turned by Nick Callahan (Owen), a doctor committed to humanitarian efforts in war-torn countries – the film could not have been more relevant to Jolie's personal journey. She had actually been sent the script in 2000, but for various reasons the project was put on hold and the film wasn't actually released until 2003. Oliver Stone, who had originally been in line to direct, dropped out over budget disagreements with Paramount, and Kevin Costner, who had agreed to take the part of Callahan, also dropped out after Jolie allegedly complained that he was too old to play her lover. The themes of the film and the issues it tackled struck a chord with Jolie, however, and, after reading the script, she realised that she wanted to know more about the UN and the work that it did. Without her persistence, said Stone, the film would never have reached production. And, according to Owen, her enthusiasm was all to do with raising awareness, 'She was very passionate about doing the film,' said Owen. 'It wasn't a vanity thing of what a fantastic part it was. It was: I want to point people towards this subject.'

As the story goes, Sarah falls in love with the rugged and

passionate Nick and is in total awe of his dedication to countries riddled with poverty and deprivation and finds it very hard to go back to her comfortable and settled London life after she has seen these places with her own eyes. Similarly, Angelina, who had spent so many years expending her energy on angst and worry and self-hatred, came to realise that all the troubles of her youth paled in comparison to the problems that people in the likes of Africa, Ethiopia and Cambodia had to deal with. 'I spent way too much time in the past locked in my own narrow world and feeling sorry about myself, instead of waking up and seeing how many advantages I have,' admitted Jolie. 'Playing Sarah taught me a lot about life and what's going on in the world. If I end up working like her in my life I'd be proud. I visited refugee camps in Namibia and spent time in a camp near the Burmese border where people had fled persecution by the government. It truly changed me.'

Angelina has always maintained that there's a part of her in every character she's played and Sarah was certainly no different. 'Sarah's not a bad person but she's not aware of many things outside of her immediate environment,' said Jolie, who could easily have been describing herself. '*Beyond Borders* changed the way I was as a person. It changed the way I see the world. Hopefully I'll become a better person as a result of the movie.' When the film came out (to bad reviews), Jolie admitted that it was actually hard for her to watch because it came so close to her own life.

When Angelina finally got custody of baby Maddox, she was filming in Africa. Starting as she meant to go on, Jolie spent every available moment with her son between takes. Unperturbed by the fact that she had 'never even changed a diaper before', the actress 'winged it' and, determined that work would not get in the way of being a mother, she entered into her new role with gusto. 'When we were filming [in Africa] I had a tent with a crib in it,' she recalled. 'From there we went to Thailand together. So my first months with Maddox were around African and Thai people. From them I learned about tying him in a sash to carry him round, feeding him and doing things their way.'

Most Hollywood actresses in Angelina's position would have hired a full-time nanny and rid themselves of all the hassle that eight-month-old babies bring, but she was determined to do the brunt of the work herself. 'I have a lot of advantages that come from my work as an actress,' admits Jolie. 'I earn very good money and can have as much support as I need. But I'm not going to be a mother who uses a nanny to do all the hard work for her. That's not going to be my work ethic as a mother.'

While Jolie had obviously prepared herself as best she could for Maddox's arrival, one thing she hadn't anticipated was being a single mother. Given that before their split she and Billy Bob had made a pact that, when one was making a film, the other would take time off so they could be together, we can only assume that she planned to have Billy with her when Maddox arrived. Their split had obviously put a stop to any plans they'd made and Angelina found herself nursing not only a baby, but also a broken heart.

At one stage during filming, Owen, whom Jolie described as 'just lovely' and a 'brilliant actor', became very concerned about his co-star's well-being. The stress of her marriage falling apart coupled with the fact that she was shooting harrowing scenes and tending to a new baby meant that she became very thin and frail. Her weight loss sparked concerns on set and Owen and the director, Martin Campbell, sat her down, expressed their fears and told her that she needed to start looking after herself properly. Their concerns were obviously appreciated and Jolie said of Owen, 'It was fantastic for me to have worked with someone like that.'

Despite her physical frailty, Jolie insists that she was 'so happy when Mad came home, there wasn't much that could have upset me'. This may have been true to a certain extent, but there's no doubt that the loss of the love of her life had affected the actress greatly and she conceded, 'The hard thing about being a parent is you don't have that other person to share the joy. I didn't plan on being a single parent, but I don't really know any other way.' The predicament she found herself in also gave her further admiration for her mother, who had raised Angelina and her brother James single-handedly. 'Now I know how my mom must have felt when my brother and I were three and one and she was 28 and by herself.'

However lonely and frightened Jolie was feeling without Billy Bob by her side, she knew that in order to be a strong and loving mother she couldn't let herself dwell too much on the past, and even started to doubt that her marriage had been all that she thought it was. 'When you're raising a child, you just blank out things that you can't deal with. Being a mother is a total commitment and you don't allow yourself the luxury of feeling sorry for yourself or whining about what went wrong in your marriage. And maybe I didn't have such a great marriage after all. Maybe a lot of it was a nice illusion.'

One of the things that she had loved so much about Thornton was his ability to make her laugh, but the camaraderie between her and her co-stars on *Beyond Borders* helped to fill this void. Angelina, who has a tendency to laugh when she is meant to be filming serious scenes, said, 'There was something about him [Owen] that made me laugh. He would say something funny and I couldn't stop giggling for the rest of the day.'

Ironically, for someone who had long been considered the most beautiful actress in Hollywood, it was having a baby – a time when most women barely even have time to look in the mirror – that made Angelina realise how beautiful she was. Never one to focus too much on the exterior of a person, this self-acceptance was undoubtedly related to the way she was feeling on the inside. Jolie felt that caring for another person unconditionally had brought her new depths and, subsequently, a new level of beauty. 'I sometimes like the way I look and sometimes don't,' said Jolie, 'but I do feel more beautiful these days than I used to, because I'm loving being a mom. I think I look my most beautiful when I'm rocking my son to sleep, it's the middle of the night, I'm exhausted and I'm covered in his dinner. One thing I've learned from motherhood is beauty definitely comes from within.'

Although she admitted that she didn't feel that sexy when she was in her 'sweatpants and changing nappies' and that she no longer had time to shave her legs, she felt more rounded as a human being and, for someone who grew up not knowing where her place was in the world or what her purpose was, she finally felt like she'd 'found all the answers'.

'I think we're all meant to do certain things – I'm meant to find my family across the world among kids who have already been born,' she said. And, while she was willing to give her all to her son, she felt like he had given a great deal to her in return. 'I am more of a woman because of Maddox,' said the actress. 'After all I've gone through, I am at last more centred and happier.'

Having been through two marriages, the whole notion of unconditional love was incredibly appealing, and, with Maddox, Angelina knew that, no matter what, they'd be there for each other. This wasn't a relationship that either of them could walk away from if it hit a rocky patch and his permanent presence in her life was obviously filling a void left by first her father and then Billy Bob. In previous years,

Jolie had positively thrived on acting on her impulses and following her (often) crazy whims, but deep down she'd been yearning for the security of something that would be there forever. And, rather than feel tied down by her new responsibility, she relished the commitment and '100 per cent focus' that having a child required. Jolie has herself admitted that even before she was famous she has never had a great deal of friends, preferring instead to either focus on whatever relationship she was in or to spend time alone. With Maddox, she had a new best friend, a constant companion and a relationship that she knew for certain was worth investing in emotionally. 'He doesn't have to love me,' said Jolie, 'and I don't have to love him, because we weren't forced together by blood. Somehow we have made the choice to be partners and if he grows up and really accepts me as a mom it's because I've earned it and not because he has to.'

Sadly for the men of this world, her blossoming relationship with her son meant that Angelina declared herself celibate, for the time being at least. The fact that her relationship with Billy Bob had been so strong and passionate yet still failed meant that she no longer trusted her romantic instincts, and she was terrified of inviting someone into her son's life in case he got attached to them. 'What if Mad spends two years getting close to a man who suddenly disappears?' she wondered aloud. 'I'm not having any kind of serious relationship because I have a son and I don't want a temporary father. I'm being very cautious. I don't know what it will take to have a man in my life. I'm just looking at the moment.' One thing she wasn't looking for, however, was another actor, and she stated that her next partner would be 'somebody who can teach me. He can make me a better person.' She also quite rightly didn't assume that a man interested in her would necessarily be interested in her son, revealing, 'I don't trust somebody being nice to Maddox just because they're dating me. I cannot imagine the kind of man I would think of as his dad.'

If Angelina missed having some male adult company in her life, she certainly wasn't going to dwell on it – the love she received from Maddox was fulfilling enough. 'I don't wallow in sadness any more,' she stated. 'I don't worry if I'm not in a relationship and I don't worry about being loved. I don't know if that qualifies me as an adult or not, but I certainly feel that my self-involved, frantic self is a thing of the past. Life involves much more than one's own selfish needs and concerns.' And luckily for Angelina, Maddox was more than happy to keep his mum company in bed at night. 'Every night I get a foot in my face or a finger in my eye,' she admitted. 'But, when he gets cosy, it's the best feeling in the world.' The actress, who had suffered from insomnia for years, also admitted that her new role as a mother had ensured that this wasn't a problem any more, revealing, 'I fall asleep hard now!'

Despite her reluctance to get involved in another

relationship at this time, Jolie was adamant that Maddox would have male figures in his life, and her brother James (whom she had grown close to again after Oscar-gate) was someone she relied on to help out with him. 'I do want him to have great male influences,' she said. 'I know a few guys in Cambodia who spend time with him. It's very important that he knows his countrymen well.'

And it was equally important to Angelina that Cambodia played a big part in the life she and Maddox shared. She was keen to put down roots there so that she could take Maddox back to his homeland regularly – whether he liked it or not. 'If he tells me when he's 19 that he doesn't care about it [Cambodia], we're going to have a huge fight,' said Jolie. 'Cambodia is part of his destiny and I will insist upon it.'

The modest two-bedroom home she had built on stilts in northern Cambodia was about as far removed from the LA mansion she shared with Billy Bob as she could have got, but, as Hollywood stars go, Angelina has a reputation for being one of the least precious, and, when she said she wanted Maddox to have a strong idea of where he was from, she meant it. As well as providing Maddox with a Cambodian base, she also loved the fact that she would have a secret hideaway that removed her from the media glare that was part of her everyday life in the States. She built the house in Samlot, which was a district often visited by missionaries and aid workers, but too off the beaten track to attract tourists. So off the beaten track, in fact, that it takes a half-hour drive down a dirt track (and through mine fields) off a main road to get there. Although Jolie was aware of the dangers she might come across living in this area, she was still horrified when she discovered that 48 landmines had been discovered on her property. As much as she wanted Maddox to embrace his culture, she was unwilling to put her baby in a potentially threatening situation and knew that she was quite literally on dangerous territory. 'I'm worried for both of us and I'm not looking for danger,' she said. 'I do question whether being there is very smart and I'm hesitant when Maddox is running around. But it's his country and he has a right to his culture. It's very important that he grows up very aware of his heritage and what is really happening in the world.' Jolie, who went on to become the patron of the Adopt-A-Minefield charity, was also wary of the wildlife and admitted that she was terrified of the tigers and bears lurking in the surrounding forest.

Eager to make friends with the locals, Angelina decided to help her neighbours – many of whom were guerrilla fighters who had been maimed by landmines – in any way she could. According to one local, 'When she first bought her house, she bought her neighbours some cows – which meant they could have milk – and rehoused a number of them in newer homes. She's now pretty legendary among the Cambodian people in this area.'

Jolie was aware that the one thing she could offer these people was financial support and she generously donated

£850,000 to fund a conservation project in the area, which aimed to preserve tens of thousands of acres of forest. Unsurprisingly, the locals were more than happy to have her in their midst. One, Hul Phany – a Khmer Rouge soldier who had lost his leg to a landmine – commented, 'I am happy she loves Samlot and helps this area – she gives a lot of money and aids wildlife.' There was one aspect of Cambodian life that Jolie was less keen to get involved in, however, and that was hunting. According to Phany, 'There is plenty of fresh meat like pork and beef to catch, but I think she prefers her own food!'

Not many of her neighbours spoke English and Jolie was keen for Maddox to grow up with a strong grasp of his native Khmer. She was even willing to learn the language herself, although this proved to be quite a challenge. 'Khmer, the language of Cambodia, is very hard but I am trying to teach him some words,' said Jolie. 'I'm not very good at it, there are something like 27 vowels – and I'm frightened! But I will learn it.' Although she was undeniably besotted with her son, and admitted that he only had to say the word 'Mumma' to get what he wanted, Jolie clearly had high hopes for her child and was determined that he would not only speak Khmer but also learn French and sign language. It was also of the utmost importance to her that he grew up realising that his mum's occupation wasn't the norm and that not many people could afford the luxuries that she could. Jolie stated, 'I plan to take him on my UN trips, so he'll have a real balance of things and understand that acting is a kind of crazy, silly side of life but that you can get lucky and sometimes make a living from it.'

With Maddox by her side, Angelina couldn't have been more content, but, in late 2003, two dramatic incidents arose to pose a threat to her happiness. The first drama occurred in October, while she was planning a UN trip to Chechnya, when she discovered that Maddox was a possible kidnap target. 'I was told not to bring my son because extremists might try to hurt him. In the end I left him behind,' said Jolie of the scare. And by December, she stood to lose Maddox a second time when it was revealed that the owner of the adoption agency she had gone through to obtain her son had been investigated and pleaded guilty to conspiracy charges. Lauryn Galindo was sentenced to 18 months in prison for money laundering and visa fraud, and Devin, her associate was sentenced on December 17, 2004 to six months of house arrest with electronic monitoring. Her sentence was less harsh because the judge determined her motivations were humanitarian, and not the pursuit of wealth. There was no evidence she knew of payments to both parents. Along with her sister and co-conspirator Lauryn Galindo, Lynn Devin had set up Seattle International Adoptions in 1997 and, up until 2001, the company had paired hundreds of Cambodian children with adoptive parents from the US. The 'cash for black-market babies' scandal emerged after the FBI shut down Devin's agency and discovered that the Galindo was receiving fees of up to $10,000 from US residents who wanted to adopt babies and then paying poverty-stricken mothers as little as $100 to give up their children. A spokesperson from the FBI commented, 'We have witnesses to the fact that some babies were not orphans but bought for peanuts from poverty-stricken parents. Mothers were paid $100 and some were ordered to pretend they were just nannies.'

Lauryn Galindo had delivered Maddox to Jolie in Africa when Maddox's adoption went through and the actress was understandably distraught to discover that the process might be under question. When Billy Bob and Angelina were awaiting custody of Maddox, the process was delayed by the fact that the US had halted all adoptions from Cambodia amid allegations of baby selling, but this had not stopped the actress in her tracks. It was only when the ban was lifted that Maddox was allowed to join his new parents.

Needless to say, Jolie spent Christmas 2003 planning a massive legal battle to keep her two-year-old son, and was determined to stop at nothing to keep him. 'My brain is obviously running over with worries,' said Jolie. 'Not just for Maddox but for all the babies and parents concerned.' But she was determined that it wouldn't come to the stage where she had to give up her son. 'I will never give my little boy back,' she stated flatly. 'I've given him a home, I've given him love, and he's mine.' The actress insisted that she had gone to 'great lengths' to ensure Maddox did not have a living birth mother in Cambodia. 'I would never rob a mother of her child. I can only imagine how dreadful that would feel. If a parent has survived, then I would want to meet them, I would want Maddox to meet them, but I have not seen any evidence that either parent of Maddox is still alive.' In fact, in previous interviews Jolie had even commented on how she thought Maddox's parents may have died, saying 'There's a very good chance it was landmines.'

Dr Kek Galabru, head of the Cambodian human-rights agency LICADHO, had this to say on the matter: 'The worst you can say is that she acted with her heart rather than her head, but I believe that the child still has at least one parent in Cambodia. I do not think he was either orphaned or abandoned, but paid for like livestock. This kind of traffic can only cause heartbreak for everyone.'

In an attempt to defend her actions, Galindo explained that it was the unclear definition of the term 'orphan' that had caused the problems. 'The Americans and Cambodians have different definitions of the 50,000 children in orphanages. American officials say both parents have to be dead to count as orphans, but in Cambodia it's enough to say they have given up or disappeared and in that poor country that is all too common.'

Much to Jolie's relief, the prosecutors eventually decided that the investigation would not change the status of any children adopted through the agency and she could rest easy knowing that Maddox was going nowhere, but the threat of losing him had driven the actress close to the edge. At one stage, she claimed that she would have moved to Cambodia permanently 'in a heartbeat' if it meant holding on to him, stating, 'I can no more imagine living without him than not breathing.'

Ironically, it was her ex-husband Billy Bob who had once warned her of such an eventuality. According to a source close to Jolie, 'Billy Bob voiced strong fears that poor Cambodian women were being taken advantage of. His doubts about the whole adoption process contributed heavily to the break-up of their marriage. Now his words have come back to haunt Angelina.'

The drama of December 2003 may have shaken Jolie, but ultimately it did nothing to put her off the idea of adoption. She had fallen in love with Maddox and it was clear that he was only the first of many children that she was going to take under her wing, with or without a partner beside her. 'There are so many lost children in this world,' said Jolie, 'and I think more people should seriously consider adoption. I feel that I've been able to fill a need in this beautiful child's world and give him all the love and devotion a mother can give.'

chapter 12

a family at war

The arrival of Maddox in Angelina's life not only saw the departure of Billy Bob, but that of her father too. Since Jon Voight left her mum Marcheline to raise Jolie and her brother alone, the father–daughter relationship had been fraught, to say the least. While he tried to see his kids when he could, and encouraged them in the best way he knew how, Voight had always fallen short in the model-father stakes as far as Angelina was concerned. Certainly, while growing up, she was much closer to her mother. Although at times she had tried to fight her feelings of resentment and establish a healthy relationship with him, it's clear that the actress never fully recovered from her father deserting his family; as a result, she was reluctant to let him into her life fully.

Although he hadn't always been around, Voight, like most fathers, was keen to have his say in the way his daughter conducted herself, how she dressed, her career choices and her love life; for the most part, however, Jolie felt that he had no right to interfere. As a child, she would often confront him while her brother tried to keep the peace, and Voight acknowledged that this was probably because they were so similar in nature – both were opinionated and fiery. Jolie had revealed that, 'In an argument, we were always very much on opposite sides,' and that this has a lot to do with the fact that she couldn't cope with the amount of pain he put her mum through. It's hard for any child to see one parent left behind by another and, from infancy, Jolie had witnessed her mum's suffering brought on by the marriage break-up.

Voight was aware of the damage his leaving had caused and admitted, 'I was having difficulties in my marriage and I had an affair. There was a lot of hurt and anger. The break-up of my marriage left emotional scars on my kids.'

While this may have been something that she tried to forgive, it was certainly something Jolie never forgot. 'My dad was always, like, one phone call away. But there are abandonment issues that stay with you,' she said.

Voight himself noticed the profound effect that his leaving had on his daughter and, in a bid to 'make up for lost time', he took Angelina on a trip to Japan when she was still a toddler. But the actor could see that, even at such a young age, something had changed inside his daughter. 'She was almost like a ghost,' he recalled. 'She wasn't there any more.

She wasn't that energised person.' Voight may have been largely responsible for his family's upheaval, but he didn't come out of the break-up entirely unscathed either. 'It was one of the toughest times in my life,' he said of his divorce. 'I was struggling to be close to my children and to be proper with their mother. I didn't feel good about myself. I was thinking about making the world a better place, yet I felt I had destroyed it in some sense.'

When she was in high school, Jolie saw a therapist but seemed dismissive of the fact that all her problems were automatically related to her parents' divorce. She did, however, acknowledge that being brought up by only one parent had made her strive for independence and, subsequently, she was reluctant to form close bonds with others. 'I don't know if my childhood was any worse than anyone else's, but it's disturbing and sad when you see one parent figure not respecting the other,' she said. 'This probably had a great effect on me wanting to be self-sufficient.'

He may not have lived with his children on a day-to-day basis, but this didn't stop Voight having opinions about the way they were being raised, and the fact that Marcheline allowed Angelina's punk-rocker boyfriend to move in with them when his daughter was only 14 was something that he had disapproved of a great deal. Like all protective fathers, Voight wanted his little girl to wear pretty dresses and remain innocent forever but instead he found Angelina to be an outspoken rebel who seemed determined to do exactly as she pleased. While he loved her spirit and could see many qualities in her that he himself had in abundance, he found her wild streak very hard to deal with. 'Both of us feel driven by the same principles,' admits Jolie, 'and each of us shares a dark, driven side that can be hard to deal with.'

Marcheline, whom Angelina described as the 'most compassionate woman I know', was both a mother and a friend to Angelina, and there can be no doubt that the absence of her father in their household meant that Angelina got away with a lot more than she would have done had Voight been around. Rather than arguing with her daughter or punishing her for rebelling, Bertrand would get upset, which only served to increase Jolie's self-hatred. 'I was raised by my mom and everything was emotional,' she said. 'Even if I would do something crazy, if I would be out all night and come back, you know, at 13, she'd cry and then I'd feel like the worst person in the world because I'd hurt my friend, my girlfriend.' As much as she hated to admit it, when it came to raising Maddox, Angelina couldn't help but notice that she had inherited her dad's strict approach. 'I've scared myself,' she said. 'I have a dad in me that's pretty hard. My dad was a nightmare and so that's all I have. I hear myself being a disciplinarian.'

While Angelina undoubtedly sympathised with her mother, she came to the conclusion that crying 'didn't solve anything' and for years found it very hard to break down, even when a role required it.

Whether she has ever meant to be deliberately provocative in interviews or not, her public honesty was another aspect of Angelina's character that her father found very difficult to deal with. As an old-school Hollywood actor, he would have preferred Jolie to be more discreet and hated her tendency to be so frank about incredibly personal matters. 'I'm really outspoken,' admits Jolie, 'and I think he has been worried about me. I've talked about, you know, everything. And just being really outspoken about my marriage [to Jonny Lee Miller], and you know, being with women, and they [the press] will take it and turn it into different things. So he's wanting me to be kind of quiet. A lot of people wanted me to be quiet during *Gia*, to not say if I'd ever done drugs, or had ever slept with a woman, which to me was being totally hypocritical. I thought it was nice to share what I had experienced, because I thought it was great. I didn't see why it was so bad.'

According to Voight's brother, Chip Taylor, it was Angelina's self-destructive nature that worried Jon the most. 'She had some drug issues and Jon was real concerned about that. And then she did all this cutting herself, and the tattoos...'

In later years, Angelina admitted her mistakes, saying that she was 'one of those terror teenagers who got a lot of repressed anger and frustration out of my system by showing the world that I didn't want to conform. It took a while, but I realised that I wasn't getting anywhere by playing the messed-up wild thing.'

It's somehow ironic that the girl Voight had named 'pretty little angel' had turned out to be what he considered a tearaway. Even at the tender age of 11, when Voight had asked his daughter to accompany him to the Oscars, Angelina was aware of the role her father wanted her to play, as opposed to who she actually was. 'I remember going to the mall and trying to find something nice we could buy,' she recalled. 'It's sort of like it was almost a character thing, like I was doing an impersonation of one of those women, looking really girlie and picking what I thought my dad would like. My dad still has his opinions about how I dress.'

Personal matters aside, Jolie had no choice but to be proud of her father's acting achievements and, when she decided to enter into the same field, Voight was genuinely pleased to discover that his daughter could more than give him a run for his money in the talent stakes. Even when she was starting out, however, with her mother acting as her manager, she was keen to distance herself from Voight for fear of being compared to him. At the age of 21, Jolie stated, 'I love my father, but I'm not him,' and she found that keeping people in the dark about her heritage took the pressure off her. 'It's far easier walking into an interview room and not [having] to be as good as Jon Voight and know that it isn't about trying to get a script to him either,' she admitted. She also felt that it would be a hindrance to her to place too much emphasis on the fact that she was following in his footsteps, saying, 'I think it's probably healthy not to put too much thought into that. It's interesting, because I think we speak to each other a lot through our work. You don't really know your parents in a certain way and they don't know you. Like, you know, he met my husband, and we'd go to dinner, but he still had his opinion of me as his daughter. So he can kind of watch a film and see how I am as a woman, the way I am dealing with my husband or the way I am crying alone.'

Interestingly, it was when she saw her father on screen that she felt she understood him the most. 'I can watch films of his and just see who he is,' she once observed.

The fact that they were in the same profession gave them welcome common ground and sometimes they would get into their latest character and show off to each other. 'Before I was about to do *Foxfire*, he was going to do *Heat* and I remember meeting him in his bedroom and showing him the butterfly knife I would carry in the film,' said Jolie. 'He came out with his bracelets and his necklace and his pinky ring and his hair extensions that he would wear in *Heat*. It was just like two kids playing dress-up.'

Having made it big early on in his career, Voight had a crisis shortly after his Oscar win in 1978, and wondered if acting was really for him. 'I don't know what I'm doing with myself,' he reflected. 'I don't know if I can do this much longer.'

Angelina had a very similar crisis after she'd finished filming *Gia*, and wondered if she had anything left to give, and it's plain to see that, for all their differences, these two were often battling the same demons. In fact, long before Angelina had even started on her humanitarian crusade, her father had been doing what he could for a number of causes. He was an advocate for American Indian rights, he'd worked on behalf of Vietnam veterans and, after making *Chernobyl: The Final Warning*, he'd become involved with the charity Children of Chernobyl, which helped children affected by the disaster.

Matt Damon, who worked on *The Rainmaker* with Voight in 1997, said of his co-star, 'Jon is one of the funnier guys you'll meet. But he also wants to talk about serious things and he has big human goals which transcend what he does for a living.'

Although Angelina has never cited her father as a direct influence in her humanitarian work, there can be no doubt that he played a part in her attitude towards those less fortunate than herself. 'He's interested in why things are the way they are,' said Jolie, 'what our responsibilities in life are.'

As an actor, Voight very much believed in quality over quantity and, although he could have raked in millions of dollars by saying yes to every movie offer that came his way, he was far too discerning to do so. As far as he could, he made films that meant something to him and had some kind of message, but his daughter struggled to do so to the same extent. As a beautiful young actress Jolie was wise enough to realise that the majority of parts thrown her way, particularly in the beginning, would require her to maximise on her looks and, for a while, she struggled to get out of the 'sexy bad girl' rut, as demonstrated by the likes of *Hackers*, *Foxfire* and *Girl, Interrupted*. Her quest for broader roles probably wasn't helped much by her public persona, and the insight into her personal life that she provided only served to increase the idea that she was dark, mysterious and obsessed with sex. This bothered Voight greatly and he yearned for his daughter to tone down her controversial statements and show the softer side to her character that he knew and loved.

Of Angelina's relationship with the press, Voight commented, 'If Angie chooses to play the bad girl, that's for her to decide. You have to make your own journey in life. Personally, I think she overdoes it. She's really not like that at all. She's a very sweet person, very loving, very bright.' He didn't have to look too far to discover where she had got her traits from, however, and knew that she was her father's daughter through and through. 'I see aspects of myself in Angie, some of my intensities,' admitted Voight. 'She has a very strong personality, which I find I have. She's a young person going through a lot of things. As a parent, you go through things with your children and that's a normal passage.'

However quick he was to fault her, Voight was fiercely proud of his daughter and went as far as to state that she was 'one of the most talented actresses of her generation'.

Unsurprisingly, he jumped at the chance to work with his daughter when she asked him to join her on the first *Tomb Raider* film as Lord Richard Croft. Given the tempestuous nature of their relationship, Jolie saw this gesture as something of an olive branch, and thought that working together would improve relations between them. 'I reached out to him,' she said. 'I thought it would be something that connected us. It was also, appropriately, about a father who was absent.'

While *Tomb Raider* isn't exactly overflowing with scenes of an emotional nature, the scene where Lara is reunited with her father is a poignant one, if only because we are aware that Jolie and Voight wrote the lines themselves. Lara says to her father, 'You let me down,' to which he responds, 'I did what I thought was right,' and we know that this is more about the actors than the characters in the film. Jolie admits that she found the filming process cathartic because she had wanted to say these words to her father in real life. 'I wrote my side, he wrote his side,' she said of the dialogue.

For a while, it seemed that her olive branch had been fruitful and, while doing interviews to promote the film, Voight positively gushed about how wonderful it was to work with his daughter and how privileged he was to join her on screen. In return, Angelina made noises about how she would be friends with Voight even if he wasn't her father and how much she could relate to him as an actor. The public declarations, as it turns out, were far removed from reality,

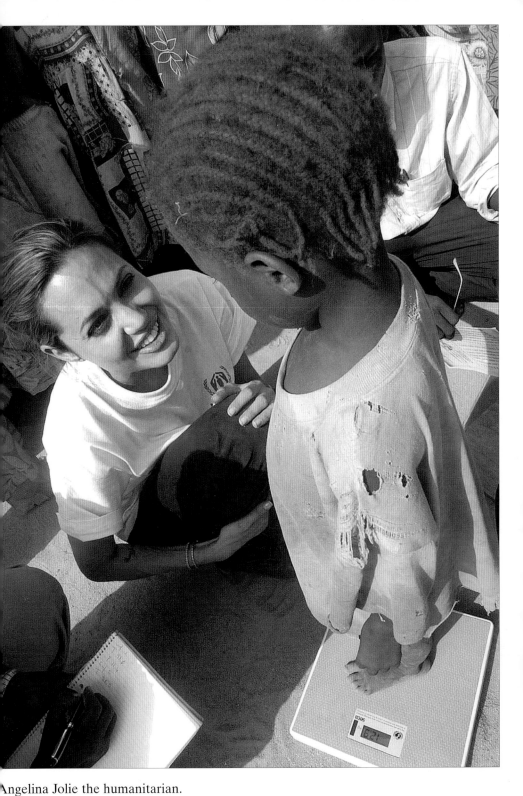

Angelina Jolie the humanitarian.

She is pictured here talking to a young refugee girl in Tine, Chad – part of her attempt
to help the refugees who have just made the treacherous journey across the scorching
desert in an attempt to escape the fighting in western Sudan.

Angelina, Goodwill Ambassador for the United Nations High Commission for Refugees, attending the annual meeting of the world economic forum, Switzerland 2005.

Above left: Enjoying some time with her son Maddox on a horse carriage ride through Central Park.

© *WENN*

Above right: Arriving in Cheshire to support the charity Adopt A Minefield, of which she is a patron.

© *Empics*

Below: Spending time sharing stories with some young Indian girls during a two day visit to New Delhi as the UNHCR Goodwill Ambassador.

© *REX Features*

A still from *Mr & Mrs Smith* – the film where Ange and Brad Pitt, two of Hollywood's sexiest actors, met. The pair immediately struck it off, and quickly rumours began to spread of problems between Brad and his then wife Jennifer Aniston (*inset*). © *WENN*

Brad and Angelina grew progressively closer as they filmed *Mr & Mrs Smith,* and, although they were nothing more than film stills, pictures of the pair getting married (*below*) made headlines in all of the tabloids.

© *WENN,* © *REX Features*

Above: With Matt Damon in the Academy Award-nominated film *The Good Shepherd*.

© WENN

Below: Brad and Angelina cruising around Ho Chi Minh City, Vietnam, on a motorbike.

© Empics

The happy family.

Angelina takes a break from filming to spend time with Brad, and her adopted children Maddox and Zahara Marley.

©*REX Features*

Inset: Proud father Brad strolls with Zahara and Shiloh on another family day out in New Orleans.

©*GoffPhotos.com*

Brad and Angelina, the most beautiful celebrity couple in Hollywood, simply can't take their eyes off one another.

and Jolie claims that their relationship went drastically downhill again after filming had finished. Voight's critical side reared its ugly head once more, this time focusing on Angelina's new pastime: UN trips. This seems absurd given his own charitable nature, but Voight felt that, by travelling to war-torn countries, his daughter was putting herself in a lot of unnecessary danger and he didn't like it. Given that Thornton was equally unenthusiastic about these trips abroad, she didn't appreciate her father's interference. 'For some reason, it was very threatening for both Billy and Jon, with this guise that they loved me and were worried about me,' she reflected later. 'But nobody volunteered to come with me...'

Just before Angelina went on one particular trip, this time to Cambodia to see a landmine for the first time, her father handed her a letter and said, 'This is my truth, this is unchanging.'

Totally unaware of what was inside, Jolie took the letter from her father, looked him in the eye and said, 'That's wonderful, I love you, see you later.'

Much to her shock and dismay, Jolie opened the letter afterwards. 'He'd written that I was a bad person,' she said. 'I was upset and thought of a hundred replies and then decided, 'I don't value this person's opinion, so it's OK.' As well as being hurt and upset, Jolie was somewhat baffled by her father's nerve. She said that the letter contained 'his opinion of some higher truth that didn't make much sense to me. He maybe thinks he knows what's best for everybody.'

It was at this stage in her life that Angelina decided that nothing would be better for her than cutting her father out of her life for good. On reading the letter, both her brother and her mother were 'very upset and very angry' at what Voight had said and, given that they knew Jolie better than her father ever had, the actress felt that cutting off all contact from him was justified. She had spent so many years trying to build bridges, trying to forget the past and trying to respect him, but his harsh words were, as far as she was concerned, totally unnecessary and unforgivable. 'He said some very ugly things to me about what he thought I was like as a person and how I was conducting my life,' said Jolie. 'At first I was completely surprised and injured by it. But then things became clear: this is a person who for the most part has been absent from my life.' Angelina defended herself further, saying, 'In all my wildness, in all my craziness, I've never done a bad thing... I'm not a bad person. To be attacked like that...'

Angelina may not have responded to Jon's letter, but Voight was now on a mission and he was willing to try anything to get through to his daughter. After they bumped into each other at a party in LA, Voight saw an opening and attempted to approach his daughter. 'I ran to give her a hug,' said Voight, 'and one of her representatives stepped in my way and said, "Get back. She doesn't want to see you."'

Unperturbed by this incident, Voight subsequently turned

up at the Dorchester hotel in London when he knew Angelina was staying there, but, again, it was a fruitless task. As soon as she laid eyes on him in the foyer, Angelina grabbed Maddox, jumped in a cab and ordered the driver to take her away as quickly as possible. The fact that the actress left her luggage on the street shows how utterly upset she was by the idea of having to converse with her father.

On an earlier occasion, Voight had managed to offend and upset his daughter by announcing to the world at an Academy Awards luncheon in March 2002 that she was adopting a child before Angelina had actually announced the news herself. 'I'm a grandfather today,' said Voight proudly. 'She got the baby in Africa.'

Thornton and Jolie had been keeping the details of Maddox's adoption quiet because they didn't want to attract any unwelcome publicity to their situation. There were already complications in getting Maddox an American visa and the fact that her dad had just drawn attention to the adoption without even thinking of the consequences infuriated Angelina. She hadn't spoken to her father for months and here he was, at a public event, being incredibly indiscreet about her private life. The fact that he told a reporter that he 'was good at diaper changes' is almost laughable considering there was no chance that he was going to be introduced to his grandson. It transpired that Marcheline, who was still very close to her ex-husband, had told him of their daughter's news, and from that day on

Angelina's mother was warned not to impart any further information about her life. Angelina did not contact her father directly after this incident but, keen to let him know how much he'd upset her, she left a 'strong message about how on the most beautiful day of my life, my first day with my son, he had cast this huge cloud'.

As we know, Thornton and Jolie split shortly after Maddox arrived and, convinced that the breakdown of her marriage had left his daughter in even greater need of psychiatric help, Voight decided that, in one final bid to get through to his daughter, he would go on live television and tell the world about her 'serious mental problems'. On 2 August 2002, a sobbing Voight appeared on the TV show *Access Hollywood* and stated, 'I don't know what else to do. I'm broken-hearted because I've been trying to reach my daughter and get her help and I have failed. I'm sorry, really. I haven't come forward and addressed the serious mental problems she has spoken about so candidly to the press over the years. But I've tried behind the scenes in every way. I've seen Angie in tremendous pain. She carries tremendous pain. I've seen that pain on her face. They're very serious symptoms of a real problem... real illness. I don't want to look back and say I didn't do everything I could. My daughter doesn't want to see me because I've made it very clear to her what the situation is and the help that she needs.'

Voight was also absolutely convinced that it was Angelina's management who were keeping him away from her because, financially, it was in their best interests to keep Angelina out of a mental institute. 'When the money train is running, everybody wants to be on it,' said a critical Voight, 'and nobody wants to make an adjustment.' He also accused his daughter of finding 'very clever ways to mask her extreme problems'.

For Jolie, the latest instalment from Voight was the final nail in the coffin of their relationship. In the past, they had managed to get through most things, but his appearance on television had ensured that, as far as Angelina was concerned, she no longer had a father. Speaking after the event, she said, 'What he did was unforgivable. He was very public about different things about me and said a lot of very harsh things. I think he's disappointed in me, but I need to stay very positive in my life, get as much accomplished, do as much as I can to be a good parent. I don't want someone around me who makes me feel bad, so I can't really afford to have a relationship with him.'

There would never have been a good time for Voight to say what he said, but Angelina was in a particularly vulnerable state and she didn't appreciate the extra drama he had created. 'To do that, considering I have a child,' said Jolie. 'To try to hurt me – right at my divorce as well... This person could have had my child taken away from me... what would that do to Mad, where would he go?' Jolie also quite rightly pointed out that, if it wasn't for his Hollywood status, no one would have paid much attention to anything

Voight had to say. 'If he wasn't a celebrity, everyone would think he was the crazy father of an actress,' she said. 'I would love to have us all psychologically evaluated and let a court decide.' For his part, Voight had the appearance of a man who was genuinely concerned about his daughter, but Jolie saw it instead as a performance and said simply, 'He's an actor.'

As a mother, Jolie was taking her responsibilities very seriously and the fact that her father had questioned her mental health when she was now responsible for another human being was what hurt her the most. He hadn't seen his daughter once since the adoption, he hadn't witnessed how well she had adapted to motherhood and how happy she was, and yet he still felt as though he was in a position to pass judgement on her mental state. 'My father had never seen me – he still hasn't – with my baby,' said Jolie. And now that she was responsible for another human being, Angelina had no doubt in her mind that there was no room in her life for such negativity. 'Like every child, Jamie and I would have loved to have had a warm and loving relationship with our dad,' she said. 'After all these years, I have determined that it is not healthy for me to be around my father, especially now that I am responsible for my own child. If you have people who put knots in your stomach, it makes you feel bad about yourself, you cry and then you get them out of your life, be strong and focus on your love elsewhere. He doesn't like so many things about me and the way I live,

I don't feel comfortable around him. I never wanted to come home and yell at Mad because I was stressed over a bad lunch with my father.'

The adoption of Maddox had obviously proved to her that blood certainly isn't thicker than water and that you don't have to love someone just because you're related to them. 'Everybody usually has a duty to spend time with people they're related to, but I don't believe it's healthy to do that just because there's a genetic connection. You've got to remember, I'm an adoptive parent so blood ties aren't what count,' said Jolie. Her travelling had also exposed her to lots of families who showed her the true meaning of unconditional love and it was clear that she thought Voight didn't exactly measure up. Jolie said, 'Doing the work I do [for the UN] I've seen fathers who have taken a bullet for their kids, so… I care for fathers in this world, just not mine.'

Remarkably, Jolie chose not to be bitter after this final dispute with her father but chose instead to let go of the past and get on with her life. 'I actually feel sorry for him,' she said. 'He's not any more to me than a man who walks down the street. I had some beautiful times with my father and I don't think he's a bad person. I don't blame him for divorcing my mother or having affairs. I just don't want to dedicate one more tear… or have to watch my mother cry one more time. I don't respect the way he treated my family as I was growing up. But I've moved on and I hope he can too. I don't believe in regret.'

And this time, Jolie meant it. Shortly after his public outpouring, she had 'Voight' legally removed from her name and she hasn't seen or spoken to her father since.

For Jon, however, there is still hope, and he maintains that one day he and Angelina will be reconciled. 'Everything I've ever done in my life since the birth of my children, every gesture and every breath I take is with their happiness in mind,' said Voight. 'I have made mistakes in my life and I've paid dearly for them.' And, contrary to what he may have said in that infamous letter, Voight has had nothing but praise for the actress since their fallout. 'I'm crazy about Angie. I love her deeply. My greatest happiness in life has been the times where I've held her hand and laughed with her. As anyone will tell you, she is the most delightful person and I am her number-one fan. One hopes that, whatever has happened in the past, we will have years of happiness ahead.'

It's been over four years, and Angelina still hasn't forgiven her father, but he can but hope...

chapter 13

return of the croft

Whether you love her or loathe her, one thing Angelina Jolie never ceases to do, in both her personal and professional life, is surprise us. Never one to conform, her film choices have been at times odd and always unpredictable. *Life or Something Like it* could easily fall into the 'odd choice' category and, in a break between *Lara Croft: Tomb Raider* and *Lara Croft Tomb Raider: Cradle of Life*, Jolie took on the purely comedic role of Lanie Kerrigan, the dizzy, blonde TV reporter who is told by a clairvoyant that she only has a week to live unless she radically changes her selfish lifestyle. Jolie has often commented that there is something of herself in every part she chooses, but, in the role of Lanie, it seems she made an exception to the rule. 'This character is everything that I find absurd about people,' she said. 'Blonde, pink lipstick, high

195

heels, and she bleaches her teeth and plucks her eyebrows. I kind of look at it as making fun of what I do for a living. And then, through a series of events, she realises that she was great when she was a dumpy teenager who loved rock and roll and didn't care what she looked like. It's about saying you don't have to try to be something you're not. And I can dig that.'

If Jolie could relate to any element of this character, it was Lanie as a teenager and she admitted that all her girlie attributes were alien to her. 'I don't shop,' she said. 'I wear the same thing every day. I've had the same shoes resoled and rezipped four times, because I won't buy another pair. I didn't even know what bra size I was until I made a movie.'

The fact that Jolie is so stingy with herself when it comes to buying clothes and yet so generous when it comes to giving huge amounts of money to charity can only be admired and sets her apart from the majority of Hollywood actresses, who spend a fortune on maintaining their pristine images. Lanie may not have been the type of girl that Angelina could relate to in any way – she rather amusingly referred to herself as looking like 'Marilyn Monroe in drag' when she donned her character's blonde wig – but the actress maintains that playing her helped bring out a feminine side of herself that she never knew existed and she also enjoyed the opportunity to show that she could do 'funny' as well as 'dark'. 'She [Lanie] is so different from who I am – and that was kind of fun. I'm drawn towards dark and unsettling characters, but there's a side of me that can be very funny and off the wall, and playing her I could be more frivolous. The message in the film is live your life and try to make the best of it; do everything as if it were your last day. It's not easy but that's a good target to aim for. That's what I'm going to do. I don't dwell on the past, I live in the day and hope for the future.'

Let's hope Jolie held on to that attitude when *Life or Something Like it* opened to mixed reviews. One particularly harsh critic carped, 'This is not one of the films you'd want to watch if you only had a week to live.'

Even the presence of the reputable Ed Burns (who plays Pete, a cameraman who works with Lanie) didn't save this film from falling into the forgettable category. That said, Jolie was commended for her 'surprising flair for self-deprecating comedy' and it was nice to see her show a different aspect of her acting talents, even if *Life or Something Like it* was the wrong vehicle.

Once she was done with Lanie, it was time for Jolie to dig out those familiar hotpants and tight vests, for she was about to take her old friend Lara Croft on some more adventures. While the first *Tomb Raider* film might not have been a huge hit with the critics, it made over £200 million at the box office and was considered a huge commercial success. As Croft, Jolie fulfilled male fantasies across the globe and there was no question that she would take on the role in the sequel, *Lara Croft Tomb Raider: Cradle of Life*.

This isn't to say that Jolie didn't have her own issues with the first film. On the contrary, the actress was more than clear about the changes she wanted to make second time around. 'We've discovered all the things we hated about the first one and where we want to make it much better,' said Jolie. 'I think we had to play a lot of things safe. I just wanted it to be a great adventure and have a character that was strong and athletic and well travelled.'

Although Simon West was no longer on board as director (Jan de Bont had taken his place), Jolie thought the sequel had a 'much better script' and subsequently the potential to be a far more sophisticated adventure than the first. She also loved the fact that the story was based on a real myth, saying, 'That makes it more interesting as opposed to something that was slightly made up. There actually is a cradle of life and you can hear it on top of the mountain [Mount Langai in Africa] – the whooshing sounds of lava are believed to be the sounds of God.'

Although she was excited to step into Croft's shorts and tank top once more, Jolie had hated the strict diet that she was put on for the first one and admitted that, for the sequel, the 'diet went out the window' and that 'other than staying away from carbs, I ate what I wanted. I had bacon, eggs and sausage this morning. A good message is to eat whatever you want, so long as it's in moderation.' Jolie described Lara as 'slimmer and sexier' second time round, but she did 'dust off the old padded bra' to ensure that Croft had her famous curves intact. While most women would be glad of a boost in the chest area, Jolie really was suffering for her art. 'I'm glad they're not really mine,' she said of Lara's ample breasts. 'I just don't find them attractive.' Fortunately for her, *Tomb Raider* fans across the globe would beg to differ.

In terms of physical training, the regime also proved to be different from the first time round, involving 'a lot of wet bike work and a lot of stick fighting', according to Jolie. The actress found that Maddox also had his uses in this department. 'Maddox keeps me pretty fit just running around with him,' said Jolie at the time. 'I use him as a weight. He's about 25lb so I lift him a lot. Doing that means I can also play with him. I have a jogging stroller so I run with him or somebody pushes him and he chases me!'

Despite being a self-confessed 'adrenalin junkie', the presence of her son on set was a constant reminder to Jolie that she was now responsible for another human being and, subsequently, she was less willing to take as many risks as she had on the first. 'I love stunts,' she said. 'I think it's a personality thing. Certain people are adrenalin junkies and I have that problem. It has often verged on being suicidal. But I've become more cautious, especially now that I have a kid. I have a responsibility to make sure that I'm going to come home each night. I can't ever be self-destructive again.' And Jolie wasn't just referring to her devil-may-care attitude towards stunts, but rather her history of self-harm. 'Before Maddox, nothing seemed real or honest enough,' she said. 'That's why I literally used to cut myself to feel pain.'

Jolie had enjoyed a fantastic working relationship with West, but, according to insiders on the set of *Cradle of Life*, relations between her and de Bont were sometimes strained, mainly due to the fact that Angelina felt he pushed her too hard. A source said, 'The pair have a cold, professional relationship. There's little warmth or camaraderie between them.'

Jolie and de Bont may not have been the best of friends on set, but her public line on him was that he was 'a brilliant director' and she seemed genuinely impressed with the course he had taken. 'The sequel really raises the stakes as far as the action sequences are concerned,' she said. And, as with the first film, she was genuinely excited about the peak physical and mental condition that the training had left her in. 'After training your body to perform in a way you never thought possible, you feel this incredible sense of control and confidence,' she said. 'I honestly feel as though I could kick anybody's ass!'

Jolie admitted that the crew had become so close while making both films that that they were 'kinda like a family' and this came as a great comfort to her at a time when she was going through her divorce from Billy Bob and coming to terms with the fact that she never wanted to see her father again. 'We all kind of struggled through the first one together,' she said. 'But... we've all become great friends. They've seen me change. It's nice.'

Both men had been a huge presence in her life during the first shoot, what with her wedding to Billy Bob taking place only five days before she landed in England to start shooting, and Voight taking the role of her father in the film. With both of them out of her life completely, the cast and crew noticed a big difference in the actress. According to one source, 'When she first got there, she was really depressed about leaving Billy Bob. She was burning up the cell-phone batteries like crazy, calling him back in the States. But now Billy Bob's not even a topic of conversation any more.'

According to Jolie, the fact that she was single enabled her to show a different, more sexual side to Lara – much to the delight of her fans across the globe, she even donned a bikini. 'When you're married, there are certain things and a certain side of you that you just can't and don't share,' said Angelina. 'It's weird, but Lara's a little sexier this time because I'm single. I felt a little freer to let loose. My sensuality and my sense of everything that's a woman is more connected.' This time round Jolie also had a lot more influence on Lara's costumes, and used the opportunity to make Croft more feminine. 'I have a lot of input and really liked her outfits this time round,' said Jolie. 'She has traditional English riding boots and a pair with "LC" branded on the side of them – I thought that was really great. It's a very girlie thing. My guns are gold this time and my bike is gold. It's a very cool look.'

For the first time in her acting career, Jolie had become a female role model through Lara Croft, something that was very important to her. She was more than used to men lusting after her, but for the first time in her acting career, she found that girls looked up to her in this role, and it was a refreshing change for the actress. 'No kids responded to any film I did before,' she said. 'So it's sweet when girls come up and show me they've done their hair the same way [as Lara]. It means a lot.'

Maddox, who was only seven months old when Jolie started working on the film, was far from neglected despite the fact that his mum was working so hard. As focused on her role as she was, Maddox remained her top priority and he spent most days on set with Jolie. He delighted in watching his mother do her stuff and, when she learned a new stunt, he was the first person she would give a demonstration too, with Jolie admitting that it was 'nice to share it with him' and that 'he had a lot of fun watching Mommy work on the set. He just finds it funny. I guess he thinks that I'm silly.'

Obviously, the set of an action film isn't always the ideal environment for a baby, so Jolie ensured that there was a room set up in Pinewood Studios for Maddox's toys so he could play there with his nanny while she got on with the job. Still new to her role as mother, Jolie was the first to admit that she wasn't always the most organised of parents, and that she often struggled to juggle everything. 'I held him every moment the cameras weren't rolling,' said Jolie. 'I lost count of the number of times he peed on my costumes.' And getting ready in the morning was no easier. 'It's just about holding him and holding his bottle, making sure his car seat's OK, that I have enough baby snacks and diapers in my bag... I'd strap on a baby papoose so I could carry him while I brushed my teeth and tried to pee... and I'd realise that I wasn't wearing a shirt – I'd forgotten to put one on before I'd put Maddox in the papoose!' she said.

Despite the chaos that his presence caused, Jolie couldn't have been more thrilled to have him around and, more than anything, he kept things in perspective for her. 'He's my priority,' she said, 'even if I'm beaten up and tired after a long day. I come home and he doesn't care what Mom's been doing all day. Why should he?'

As heartbroken as she was when she split with Billy Bob, it seemed that the love she shared with Maddox was proving to be much more fulfilling than the obsessive relationship she had enjoyed with Thornton; and, when Jolie said that she was a lot happier in herself and more satisfied with her performance on the second film than the first, there can be no doubt that this was down to her son. 'Everybody wants to feel useful. I was never fulfilled just as an actress. I think [being a mother] has made me a better actress.'

On the whole, the *Cradle of Life* shoot went smoothly, but it certainly wasn't without its dramatic moments. Jolie recalled one particularly hairy scene. 'I was riding a horse trying to fire the shotgun at the same time. Because I'm left-handed, when the gun went off the casing came out and hit me in the eye. I guess it's designed for a right-handed person. It was a big scare.'

Jolie was equally shaken when, while she was filming some scenes in north Wales, Maddox scalded himself on a boiling kettle. A frantic trip to Liverpool's Alder Hey Children's Hospital ensued and he was treated there for minor burns. Touched by the excellent treatment and care that he received from the staff there, Jolie donated £50,000 to the hospital and Maddox has been an avid Liverpool FC fan ever since. 'He loves football,' said Jolie of her son. 'And he has his own Liverpool kit. But they say he has a rugby body, he's more of a scrum half, whatever that means. But I don't want him to play rugby, I don't want him to get hurt!'

Ironically, Billy Bob is also a huge Liverpool supporter, but Maddox's choice of team has little to do with the father that he never knew.

Filming the second *Tomb Raider* film gave Angelina a chance to reacquaint herself not only with Lara Croft, but also with England, the country she had loved since she had made *Hackers* almost ten years earlier. Pinewood Studios had become something of a second home to the actress and, now that she was a mother, she felt more at home in England than ever.

Following her split with Billy Bob, Angelina said that she

looked at Maddox and said, 'Well, honey, we can go anywhere in the world. Where would you like to go?'

Despite being a huge Hollywood star, Jolie had never really liked LA and had only moved there from New York when she married Billy Bob because his children were based in LA and he understandably wanted to be near them. Now that she had severed all ties with him, Jolie could live anywhere she wanted and, as far as she was concerned, there was no better place to raise a child than England. 'I love England,' said Jolie. 'One day [during filming], I was watching Maddox playing in the garden and he looked so happy and serene. I looked at him and thought, "We need a home, we need a backyard, let's do it tomorrow."'

While filming, Jolie rented the very same £2.1 million, eight-bedroom luxury converted farmhouse (set in 300 acres with a swimming pool and tennis courts) that Tom Cruise and Nicole Kidman had lived in when they were filming Stanley Kubrick's *Eyes Wide Shut*. Jolie decided that she would like to buy the property, located near the village of Fulmer in Buckinghamshire, from the owners and make it a base for her and Maddox. 'I feel so much more connected to the rest of the world when I'm there,' she said of her new home. 'I get access to what is going on globally. Maddox and I can go out all the time. We choose to live a normal life and that's easier in England. When you don't put on the star attitude, you can live your own life.'

The anonymity that living in the UK afforded the star was

no doubt a large part of the appeal and, having felt like she'd had a very sheltered and one-sided education in the States, she liked the idea of Maddox growing up in a country which she considered to be more politically and socially aware. As an A-list star, her every move in LA was followed, not to mention photographed, by the paparazzi, and, as the mother of a young son, she wanted to escape this media scrutiny. Jolie found that living out in the sticks in Buckinghamshire made for a much quieter life and removed her and Maddox from the media spotlight. As is the case with many celebrities, Jolie was fiercely protective of her son and felt that he had the right to a normal upbringing as much as any child, that he shouldn't suffer just because of what his mum did for a living. When asked about the difference between life in the States and life in the UK, Jolie said of the UK, 'I tend to go to nice dinners more and have nice tea. Also, life just shuts down and it is more quality time with other people here. It seems to be more about family – more going to the park with the kid.'

The education system in Britain appealed to Jolie too, and she started researching schools for Maddox who, she admitted, 'sounded a bit English' when it came to saying his first words. She dreamed of sending him off to school in the morning in a nice little uniform and found that, while she was sat in the make-up chair at work, her mind would wander off and she'd think about the times to come, when she'd have to take part in things like the egg-and-spoon race on school sports days. When the day actually came for Maddox to start school, his mum had an uncharacteristic crisis of confidence and worried about how she would compare to the other mothers. On one occasion, when she was meant to be attending a parent/teacher night, she had to change the appointment three times because she was so apprehensive. 'I remembered being sent to the principal's office, so the idea made me nervous,' admitted the actress. 'I suddenly thought, "Do I have my tattoos covered up? Do I have too much eyeliner on?"'

And it wasn't only her own appearance she had to worry about. Maddox, who had been sporting a mohican since he'd had hair long enough to style into one, was banned from wearing a particular piece of jewellery he loved because it didn't comply with the regulation uniform. While Jolie had admitted that she was excited about her son getting a great education in England, she wasn't quite prepared for the fact that her son would be discouraged from standing out from the crowd, at least in terms of appearance. 'He had a helicopter necklace but that's not OK in England,' said Jolie. 'They downplay the individual, which is kind of a problem.'

With Maddox in tow, Jolie, who was undoubtedly still recovering from the breakdown of her marriage, was adamant that she wasn't looking for a new relationship. She maintained that introducing anyone to Maddox as a potential father figure was too much of a risk and thought that it was easier, for the time being at least, to remain single. 'As much as I seem really wild, I take somebody invading my personal space very seriously,' she said.

Clearly damaged by her last relationship, she stressed that marriage was not her 'cup of tea' and that she didn't have 'faith in the permanence of relationships'. This is not to say that Angelina ruled out ever having a relationship again. On the contrary, she said she was 'looking forward to the day when all that is there again. I'd love to find that friend in life that has a boundless will and energy and strength for something remarkable.'

For all her protestations about being single, however, it was no secret that Angelina saw her time in England as an opportunity to become close once more to her first husband, Jonny Lee Miller. And it wasn't long before the two were spotted out and about on the town together, looking a lot cosier than divorcees normally would. But then, for anyone who had followed Jolie's love life avidly, this rekindling of an old flame would have come as no surprise.

Unlike the bitterness and disappointment she displayed when she split up with Billy Bob, Angelina had never had a bad word to say about Jonny. She had loved him deeply, but she had been too young for marriage and she took full responsibility for the fact that their union didn't last, blaming herself and her need to grow as a person. Miller obviously didn't bear any grudges, despite the fact that Jolie had broken his heart, and the pair kept in touch over the years and remained friends. 'We never really fell out,' said Jolie. 'And neither of us wanted a divorce. It was just a set of circumstances with him wanting to be in one place and me wanting to be in another. We stayed friends and our friendship is growing again, all the time.'

But this 'friendship' that she spoke of had the appearance of something far from platonic: the pair were spotted kissing in public several times and even pictured getting tattoos together (Jolie had 'Know your rights' written between her shoulder blades) in a parlour in LA in February 2004.

When asked about her renewed relationship with him, Jolie said, 'Jonny's a wonderful guy. Of course we're close. I hope it will remain that way.' Miller himself commented that Jolie had 'mellowed a little' since he'd last been involved with her, but wouldn't be drawn on whether or not they were getting back together. As it turns out, any rekindled romance would come to nothing. More than anything, it seems that, at a time when she was lonely, vulnerable and unwilling to risk getting involved with anyone new, Miller had been a shoulder to cry on for Jolie. She had always been able to rely on him when they were together, and it was a great comfort to the actress that she still could. Whether Miller had fallen in love with his ex-wife all over again and wanted their reunion to be more permanent is anyone's guess, but, as far as Jolie was concerned, this wasn't on the cards. 'I would like to tell Jonny that I love him,' she said. 'But I think he knows. I'm going to be so happy as he finds all the happiness in the world. I am grateful to him for being such a great husband when we were married.'

Unlike the disappointment she felt after seeing the first *Tomb Raider* film, Jolie was pleased with the way the second one turned out (even though it was a total failure at the box office), and subsequently felt that her work with Lara Croft was done. She had given all she had to give, and, despite initially stating that she would work on a third film if the script was right, Jolie had changed her tune by the end of the *Cradle of Life*. 'I wanted to do a sequel because I wasn't happy with the first movie,' said Jolie. 'I'm much happier with the second film. We made a film we should have made the first time. I don't feel the need to do that again.'

And so Jolie had decided to hang up her tank tops, hotpants and guns and lay to rest the character that had secured her status as one of the sexiest female actresses in the world.

chapter 14

alexander

Never one to shy away from a predominantly male cast, Jolie signed up for *Taking Lives* soon after she'd finished the second *Tomb Raider* film, and found herself starring alongside Ethan Hawke, Olivier Martinez and Kiefer Sutherland. The film was based on the novel of the same title by Michael Pye and was about a successful FBI profiler Illeana Scott (Jolie) who is summoned to hunt down a serial killer who assumes the identity of his victims. Jolie does a good job as the smart, sexy yet vulnerable Scott and her male co-stars don't let her down in this thriller. As usual, the film didn't hit the headlines because of its outstanding direction or fantastic performances, but rather because of the fact that Jolie was romantically linked to not one but all three of her co-stars. 'The amount of people I'm dating at the moment – it's physically impossible,' said Jolie, who was still single after her split from Billy Bob. 'We started to joke about it because it was said I had dated the whole cast. Kiefer, Ethan, Olivier – we were all laughing about it. But I got annoyed about the rumours over Olivier because he has a girlfriend [Kylie Minogue] he is very close to, so that implies something bad.'

At one stage, Minogue felt so threatened by Jolie's friendship with the French actor that she flew out to the set to make sure her partner was behaving himself. But then Kylie wasn't the first girlfriend or wife who had shuddered at the thought of her loved one working with such a renowned seductress. Jolie may have laughed off such rumours, but it seems that, in the case of Ethan Hawke, who was still married to Uma Thurman at the time, there might have been something in the reports. Pictures of Jolie and Hawke kissing between scenes in July 2003 sparked rumours of an affair and Ethan's public declarations of admiration for the actress only added fuel to the fire. 'Every now and then God gets it exactly right,' Hawke told one journalist. 'She's ravishingly beautiful and never gets old and never gets boring. She is a really incredible woman, and I liked her.' Hawke even admitted that he found he had more friends than he thought when he was making *Taking Lives*, because they all wanted to visit him on set and get a glimpse of Jolie.

Angelina never admitted to a fling with the married father of two, but did return the compliment. 'Ethan is a wonderful, good man and a great father,' she said.

Jolie's next two films were refreshingly free of scandal and, in *Sky Captain and the World of Tomorrow*, she teamed up with her first husband's best friend, Jude Law. When Jolie first met Jonny Lee Miller, he was sharing a flat in London with Jude and Ewan McGregor so there was no chance of Angelina falling for her co-star here. The film, a science-fiction adventure, is set in New York City in 1939. It is one of the first movies to be shot entirely on a digital backlot with actors in front of a bluescreen; all the sets and nearly all of the props were computer-generated, and Jolie, who plays Frankie, admits that she found it very hard to get used to initially. 'At first it felt very silly and then I think that it's great to get back to what's fun about this business,' she said. 'It's creative and you try things that aren't safe and be silly again and be bold with your choices. It's refreshing.' Jolie said it was 'nice to finally work with Jude' and was surprised how well she got on with another of the film's stars, Gwyneth Paltrow. 'Gwyneth is very funny. I had never met her before and she's great, we got on really well. You always hear weird things when actors come together but we all had a great experience.'

Jolie followed *Sky Captain* with another break from tradition and agreed to be the voice of Lola in the DreamWorks animation film *Shark Tale*. This project appealed to Jolie because it was something that she thought Maddox would enjoy, but her mother Marcheline was a little distressed that yet again her daughter had been cast as a temptress. Lola is the femme fatale of the ocean and comes between the hero Oscar (Will Smith) and his long-suffering girlfriend Angie (Renée Zellweger). 'Why would they cast you as the bad fish?' enquired Marcheline. 'Why didn't they make you the angelfish? Your name is Angie.'

Jolie replied, 'Because, mom, the world doesn't see me as you see me.'

Despite her mum's reservations, Angelina insisted that making *Shark Tale* was 'a lot of fun – it's such a laugh to see yourself as an animated fish!'

Alexander, Jolie's next film, was a far more serious affair, however, and again, it would gain more publicity for what was going on off set than on.

When Angelina signed up to star in Oliver Stone's biopic *Alexander* with fellow Hollywood hellraiser Colin Farrell, it was obvious that sparks were going to fly between the pair. Like Angelina, Farrell has a reputation as one of the wildest actors in Hollywood and, before going into rehab in December 2005, rumoured to be receiving treatment for an addiction to recreational drugs (although the official line was that he was suffering from 'exhaustion and a dependency on prescription medication'), he had a reputation as a womanising party animal. Born in Dublin on 31 May 1976, Colin was a year younger than Angelina and, although his film career began in 1999 with his appearance in *The War Zone*, he didn't become well known until he appeared in box-office hits such as *The Recruit*,

S.W.A.T. and *Phone Booth* in 2003. In 2001, he married the English actress Amelia Warner after a whirlwind romance but the couple separated after only four months together. Following his divorce, Farrell took full advantage of his sex-symbol status and enjoyed a string of flings with a host of beautiful women – one of whom was rumoured to be Britney Spears – and admitted that he regularly employed the services of high-class call girls. Farrell also admitted that he had a fairly lax attitude towards the use of contraception, which might explain how one of his many girlfriends, Kim Bordenave, fell pregnant while they were together. Model Kim gave birth to Farrell's son in September 2003 and, although the couple split before James was born, the actor continues to see and support his son, citing him as the most important person in his life. In fact, his stint in rehab is said to have been inspired by his desire to sort himself out for James's sake.

Jolie and Farrell were very similar in the sense that they were rebels who lived life by their own rules, but they also had a very sensitive, intense and passionate side to their characters. Like Jolie, Farrell had also suffered from insomnia and bouts of depression while growing up and it became quickly apparent when they met on the *Alexander* set in Morocco that they had a lot in common. Farrell had fancied Jolie since seeing her in *Tomb Raider* and when he got to know the actress he found that she more than lived up to his expectations. In short, Farrell had met his match.

When it came to casting the biopic – based on the life of Alexander the Great, who conquered almost all of what constituted the known world by the age of 25 and died aged 33 – Stone knew that he needed someone strong to take on the role of Alexander's mother, Olympias, and, having admired Jolie since he saw her performance in Gia, the director was certain that he wanted Jolie on board. 'A lot of modern actresses play the polite middle, but, with Angelina, you have more of the Bette Davis tradition,' said Stone. 'She goes for it in a strong, determined way, and it's rare to see that with young actors.' He also described her as a 'natural born actress'.

Given that Farrell had agreed to take on the role of Alexander, Stone's decision to cast Jolie as his mother didn't seem like the natural choice, and Jolie had her doubts about it as much as anyone else. She trusted that Stone knew what he was doing, however, saying 'when he casts people, he casts their spirit' and liked what he had done with the script and the fact that there were 'great scenes that talk about life, power, passion and murder' but still she was hesitant about playing Colin's mother. 'I wasn't sure how that was going to work,' she admitted. 'I met with Oliver and Colin and we all kind of said, "We're either going to be criticised and attacked for this, or it's right and it should happen." So we took a really big chance. But I think, seeing us separately, he fits Alexander and I fit Olympias and somehow together we became mother and son.'

With her long tumbling locks, exotic looks and luxurious costumes, Jolie certainly looked the part, but that's not to say that she didn't find it challenging to portray the Greek queen. 'You're doing a period piece and doing an extreme character, ageing, and accents and high emotions,' she said. 'There's such an easy tendency to go over the top and make a caricature of the person. So to just keep it subtle and find her heart and her reality [was a challenge].' Some might say the film was something of a 'challenge' to watch, and the critics completely panned it, with one describing it as 'an honourable failure'. The general consensus was that it was more of a history documentary than an action film – and an inaccurate documentary at that. While Jolie is undoubtedly very easy on the eye as the incredibly powerful and dominant Olympias, there is something uncomfortable about her performance, which isn't helped by her laboured Arabic accent. One critic even described her as being like a 'grand diva out of a medieval soap opera'.

Criticism aside, there's no doubt that Jolie enjoyed herself on the film and she was particularly pleased to play a more mature woman. 'It's nice to be hired for something where I'm not the sexy wife,' she said. 'I'm in the film for other reasons.' Totally unfazed by the fact that Olympias spends much of the film draped in snakes, Angelina, who had kept serpents as pets in the past, even went to the lengths of spending extra time with the creatures between scenes, just so she could 'get to know them'. She also enjoyed the fact that she had to age throughout the film, saying, 'I think age is beautiful. I actually like the thought of it.'

Although Jolie described the dominant, controlling and incredibly sexual Olympias as 'psychotic', she had a great deal of affection for her and, as was the case with a lot of the parts she played, she found she could relate to her on some level. 'I loved her!' she admitted. 'If I lived at that time with the dangers, threats and the lack of power that she had as a woman, I wouldn't have been that different from her. I saw her as a mother who really would push her son at a time that, if he didn't get the throne or acquire a certain strength, ability and greatness, he would just die or be exiled. That made it easy for me to think about my own son and what he'd have to do to protect himself from things that could hurt him.' In one particular scene, where Olympias learns of her son's death, Jolie tried to draw on her experience as a mother but found that it was too upsetting. 'I sat there in a corner for five minutes and I cried and screamed so hard,' said Jolie. 'It was so hard for me that, in the end, I gave up. I just didn't want to go there. I didn't care if it was a bad scene, I just didn't want to go there. If anybody did anything to my son in real life, I would kill them.'

With his distracting blond wig and inappropriate Irish accent, Farrell's performance was as baffling and confused as Jolie's, but their on-screen relationship is undoubtedly intense, both physically and emotionally. And, even though they play mother and son, the sexual tension between them is so strong that it gives Oedipus a run for his money. Jolie put this down to the fact that both she and Farrell have similar methods when it came to getting into character, saying, 'It's funny, because he and I both pace. In between takes to keep my energy up and stay focused, I pace. And Colin paces – we found, when we'd pace around, we kept running into each other. It was really funny. Then when they'd say action we'd come at each other.'

And, as was the case with Jolie and several of her former co-stars, this intensity continued off screen, and subsequently it was her 'close friendship' with Farrell that grabbed more headlines than the film itself.

While Jolie and Farrell have never admitted to having a sexual relationship, they were very open about their admiration and affection for one another, and there was much evidence to suggest that at times their relationship wasn't strictly platonic. Jolie acknowledged the attraction between them and said that they did consider getting involved romantically, but decided it wouldn't be a good idea. 'We were too similar,' she explained. 'We talked about a relationship but it isn't the right thing to do for us. Colin is a fascinating and attractive guy. But we'd be too intense for each other.'

Farrell was no less gushing about his co-star, and was particularly taken with her skills as a parent. 'She is gorgeous when she is with her baby, and really inspiring,' he said. 'She's been giving me tips on being a good parent. I love watching her with Maddox.' He was also aware of the similarities between them and said that it was 'ironic' that she played his mother in *Alexander*. 'We are really, really alike,' said Farrell. 'I don't believe in all that fucking hocus pocus, but we are both Geminis. Maybe we are more twins than the same person. I've never met anyone who has so much going for her who is also so selfless. Angie is so open-hearted. And so very, very honest. She's amazing.' As if this wasn't enough, Farrell also described Jolie as his 'ideal woman'.

Unsurprisingly, Farrell wasn't the only man on the set of *Alexander* who took a fancy to Jolie; Val Kilmer, who played King Philip II of Macedonia, the husband of Olympias, was quite open about the fact that he loved every minute of his sex scenes with the gorgeous Jolie. 'My role consisted mostly of sharing a bed with Angelina Jolie and throwing her around in it, which is about as much fun as it is possible for a man to have,' said Kilmer. 'Don't tell her or Oliver Stone this but, when we were doing the really sexy bits, I kept messing up my lines on purpose... so we would have to do it again. I spent four months doing that... and someone paid me millions of dollars for the pleasure.'

While rumours abounded that these two were also dating, Jolie saw him as more of a father figure than anything else. 'We're both really sensitive and nice to each other,' she said of Val. 'It's great. I've not had the father to say, "Let me guide you a little bit about the kind of things I think you'd be interested in and how to do it."'

Despite Farrell and Jolie's insistence that they were 'just good friends', they were spotted on more than one occasion getting up close and personal in a string of London bars and hotels in late 2003, after filming had finished. Speculation that they were in fact an item became rife, when, in December of the same year, Colin accompanied Angelina and Maddox on a Christmas trip to the pyramids in Egypt. Although they took separate planes to Cairo on Christmas Eve and checked into their hotel under false names, paparazzi shots of the couple cuddling and taking camel rides together confirmed their closeness and, together with Jolie's son, they looked like a tight family unit. At this time, Angelina was dealing with Maddox's adoption scandal and, if nothing else, the Irish actor was more than happy to lend her his support and a shoulder to cry on.

Perhaps one of the reasons that Jolie was reluctant to commit to a relationship with Farrell was his love of partying, and it's thought that she wanted more stability than he could give. Now that she had Maddox to think about, she was determined that her next serious relationship would be committed and secure and Farrell's wild ways didn't exactly make him ideal father material. In fact, the actress is said to have put a stop to their fling when she saw pictures of him out drinking and looking cosy with other women.

The fact that he wasn't right for her as a long-term partner didn't seem to lessen Jolie's affection for Farrell, however, and, more than anything, she sounded maternal towards him when she talked about him in interviews. There's no doubt that they had bonded over similar past experiences, and the fact that they were both such free spirits. Throughout the filming of *Alexander*, Jolie felt as if she had watched Farrell grow up. '[The tough role] helped him become more of a man,' she reflected. 'I know it was hard… and he was allowing all his demons to come through… but I was kind of secretly sitting in the corner, excited, happy for his pain, knowing that it would make him grow.'

Angelina may not have admitted to an affair with Colin but she did reveal that, after a period of celibacy post-Billy Bob, she was ready to resume her sex life. She knew that her next serious relationship would have to be right given that a child was now involved and figured that her inability to find the right long-term partner should not get in the way of her fulfilling her physical desires. In typically frank fashion, Angelina discussed in a series of interviews how she had taken on two lovers, both of whom knew that their relationship with her was purely sexual. 'I've got physical desires,' she said. 'That's all I'm thinking about right now – but I don't want a boyfriend or a husband.' The fact that she never revealed the identity of the men she was sleeping with enabled the press to speculate even further about the nature of her relationships with the likes of Colin Farrell, Ethan Hawke and even Jonny Lee Miller. There was also a rumour that she was seeing a millionaire Italian businessman named

Daniele Patini. 'I went for about two years with absolutely no man around me and then decided to get closer to men who were already close friends,' she said. 'It's an adult way of having relationships. As crazy as it sounds, meeting a man in a hotel room for a few hours and then going back and putting my son to bed and not seeing that man again for a few months is about all I can handle.'

Although she never mentioned any names, Jolie did state that one of the men was someone she had actually been attracted to while married to Billy Bob. 'When I was married to Billy, I met a man I never slept with,' she said. 'We had dinner once and it ended up being, "Look, I'm married, I can't sleep with you. I can't even finish dinner, 'cause it's uncomfortable."' Three years later, Angelina called him and suggested that they started a no-strings physical relationship. 'We spent a couple of dinners discussing the details of how this was actually going to happen. It was fascinating,' revealed Jolie.

She may have been clear about what she wanted, but it took the men a while to get used to the idea. After all, it's not every day you get one of the most beautiful women in the world asking you to have sex with her and not to call her afterwards. 'Usually there's a stereotype that women have to give their hearts in relationships while men can just give their penises. But I don't believe that,' she said. In fact, if anything, it was the other way round and one of Angelina's lovers wound up wanting more, even asking to meet her son Maddox.

As much as she enjoyed her sojourns in hotel rooms with these men, where they 'watched the news, talked about life', she didn't want either of the relationships to spill over into her family life. 'Have safe sex and you don't confuse your family and you don't confuse someone else's family,' was her mantra, and she stuck to it. That is until she met a certain actor on the set of her next movie...

Chapter 15

an affair to remember

From the time they got together on a blind date in
1998, Brad Pitt and Jennifer Aniston were crowned
as the golden couple of Hollywood. As Rachel Green in the
hugely popular sitcom *Friends*, Aniston had become one of
America's best-loved actresses and, when she paired up with
the equally successful, beautiful and talented Pitt, the media
world couldn't have been more excited. Pitt and Aniston
may have been hugely wealthy and two of Tinseltown's most
sought after A-list stars, but both actors had a down-to-
earth air about them which made them an incredibly
likeable couple. To outsiders, they seemed absolutely perfect
for each other and, from day one, celebrity fans across the
world were rooting for their happiness. Pitt was (and still is)
one of the most desired actors on the planet, but no one
resented Aniston for taking him off the shelf.

Unlike Jolie, whom some women can't relate to and may subsequently feel threatened by, Aniston is the kind of approachable girl-next-door type that you could imagine inviting round for a cup of tea and a chat. In *Friends*, she played a funny, caring, self-deprecating shopaholic and, after being the show was on air for ten years, it became more and more difficult for the public to separate the character from the actress, particularly given the close relationships she enjoyed with her fellow cast members. Jolie has always been open about the fact that she enjoys few close friendships, particularly with women, whereas Aniston has had the same close-knit group of friends for years, most of whom she knew before becoming famous. This isn't to say, however, that Aniston was something of a Plain Jane. Since the first episode of *Friends* aired in 1994, she had, with the help of her famous 'Rachel cut' and petite curves, become an international pin-up. While Courteney Cox Arquette (Monica Gellar) and Lisa Kudrow (Phoebe Buffet) were undeniably beautiful actresses, it was Aniston who always came out on top in the 'most-fancied' polls and was often named as the 'Friend' most men would want to date. Before being set up with Pitt by their agents, Aniston had her fair share of high-profile romances with the likes of Counting Crows singer Adam Duritz and actor Tate Donovan (who later went on to star in *The OC*), but none of them ever attracted as much attention as her union with Pitt. After dating for two years (Aniston has said they had 'so much fun falling in love'), she and Pitt got engaged and had a $1 million fairy-tale wedding in Marcy Carsey's (a producer on *Friends*) Malibu mansion on 29 July 2000. Complete with 200 guests, four bands, a gospel choir, champagne, lobster and fireworks, the ceremony was a lavish affair and the only break from tradition was the wedding vows. Favouring the personal touch, the couple added some of their own to the proceedings, with Aniston promising to make her husband his favourite banana smoothies and Brad promising to regulate the thermostat in their home. The guest list was celeb heavy with Aniston's *Friends* co-stars in attendance along with Cameron Diaz, Ed Norton (Pitt's *Fight Club* co-star), Salma Hayek and singer Melissa Etheridge.

The couple went to great lengths to keep it a private affair but, in order to satisfy the appetite of the fascinated public, they issued one official black-and-white photograph from the day. Resplendent in her beautiful Lawrence Steele wedding dress, Aniston looked a picture of happiness as she adoringly gazed at her handsome husband and the general consensus was that this would be one of the rare showbiz marriages that would have a happy-ever-after ending.

Appearances can be deceptive, though, and, despite the fact that their fans had Jen and Brad on a pedestal, the actress was always fairly open about the detrimental effect her parents' divorce had had on her and how she never quite believed in the idea of a perfect marriage. Actor John

Aniston and Jen's mother Nancy Dow divorced when the actress was nine and, although Jen appeared to have the world at her feet, there was a deep-rooted insecurity within her that refused to go away. She admitted that she often experienced 'fear, mistrust, doubt and insecurities' in her marriage and confessed, 'When your parents split up it's impossible to delude yourself about fairy-tale marriages and happy endings.' Lacking in self-esteem, Jen once said that it was only when Pitt fell in love with her that she even started to like herself and it's clear that, although he adored his wife, there were a lot of issues that Pitt had to help her work through.

Brad himself had come from a stable, middle-class background and his parents William and Jane Pitt, who still live in his hometown Springfield, Missouri, remain happily married after many years together. While Brad enjoyed a close relationship with his parents and two siblings Doug and Julie, Aniston – who has two half-brothers, John Melick and Alex Aniston – became estranged from her mother Nancy in 1999 when she wrote a book about her daughter entitled *From Mother And Daughter To Friends*. Aniston had long disapproved of her mother speaking out about her daughter's life in interviews (much in the way that Angelina disapproved of her dad for being similarly indiscreet), and when Nancy published the book about her in 1999 it was the final straw. Not only was she struck off the wedding list but Nancy never even got to meet her son-in-law. This was one of the many areas of his wife's life that Brad attempted to help Jen work through, but in this particular instance he was unsuccessful. In fact, Aniston only made contact with her mother again after her marriage to Brad collapsed.

For a while, Brad and Jen looked to be living in marital bliss, and, in rare breaks between filming, the pair were often pictured taking romantic trips abroad and travelling the world together. They shared a $14 million mansion in Hollywood, and Brad, who has a keen interest in architecture, spent a great deal of time renovating the property in order to create the perfect marital home. Many showbiz couples find that their relationships are thwarted by professional jealousy, but this never seemed to be a problem for these two and they were incredibly supportive of each other's career. Brad even made a guest appearance in the 2001 Thanksgiving episode of *Friends* and, if Jen wasn't accompanying him on the red carpet for one of his many film premieres, he was escorting her to award ceremonies. Aniston won both an Emmy (2002) and a Golden Globe (2003) for her portrayal of Rachel in *Friends* and no one could have been prouder than her husband, even if she did forget to mention him in her Golden Globe speech. Despite the fact that Brad's blossoming film career led to him starring opposite a host of incredibly beautiful actresses, Aniston maintained that she never felt threatened by his co-stars. 'I had a period in my life when I was younger when I was jealous, but I don't feel that now,' she said. 'He's very loyal; he's not impressed with that sort of stuff. So thankfully I'm not a model!' Ironically, Jen was so secure in her relationship that, on the one occasion when she met Angelina Jolie before filming for *Mr. & Mrs. Smith* had begun, she said, 'Brad is so excited about working with you. I hope you guys have a really good time.'

Little did she know that the 'good time' Jolie would have with her husband would eventually lead to the demise of her marriage.

For the time being, however, the world's media assumed that all was well in the marriage and chose to focus on the topic of children and the couple were continuously asked if and when they were planning to extend their family. In 2001, a year into their marriage, Brad talked openly about the couple's baby plans, saying, 'I believe in the concept of marriage and family and it has always been my intention to take this step and build a life with someone.' He also went on to say that he was ready for fatherhood and dreamed of having daughters. 'I finally think I'm at a place where I won't mess a kid up too much,' he said. 'I want little versions of Jennifer, It's my dream.'

Jen was similarly positive on the subject and said that she was 'absolutely' keen to start a family. However, with every year that Jen signed a new contract for *Friends*, the baby plans were put on hold and it was widely believed that, as soon as the show ended in 2004, the couple would attempt to conceive. Jen added fuel to this fire by saying that after the last series was over she was going to take a long holiday and 'then it's about family'.

By this stage, however, cracks had started to show in their relationship and in a series of interviews the couple seemed rather less besotted with each other than they had done in previous years. In early 2004, Brad said, 'Nothing is ever what it seems, is it? I hate the notion of fairy tales anyway. No one can live up to such a thing. Marriage is tough, it's not easy. There is so much pressure to be with someone forever and I'm not really sure if it's in our nature to be with someone for the rest of our lives.' He also told *Vanity Fair* magazine that he and Jen didn't 'cage each other with this pressure of happily ever after' and, while promoting *Troy* in the April of that year, told one journalist, 'Neither of us wants to be the spokesman for happy marriage, for coupledom. I despise this two-becomes-one thing, where you lose your individuality.'

It can be no coincidence that Brad made all these comments shortly after becoming acquainted with Jolie on the set of *Mr. & Mrs. Smith*, the film which he had personally talked her into doing, and it's clear that after becoming close to the actress he started to doubt that his marriage would last forever. The Hollywood rumour mill naturally went into overdrive and many suggestions were made that Jolie and Pitt had fast become a lot more than just good colleagues. Insiders from the set of their film commented on the fact that Brad had not only taken a shine to Angelina, but had also become hugely attached to Maddox and the actor allegedly spent many hours between filming bonding with him. 'There was a platonic relationship going on,' said an actor from the set. 'They often relaxed on a patio that Pitt set up outside his trailer. We called it Brad's Grotto. Quite often Brad and Angelina were out there while the little boy was playing in the grotto.'

Rumour has it that, in the second stage of filming (there was a break in between so Brad could go off and film *Ocean's 12*), Brad and Angelina even had adjoining hotel rooms. Another telling remark from the actor which suggested he was no longer in love with his wife was when he described his marriage to Jen as 'an extraordinary friendship' and said that they had made a pact to 'see where this relationship is going. I'm not sure it really is in our nature to be with someone for the rest of our lives just because you made this pact.'

Jen was similarly non-committal when it came to discussing her relationship and, when asked by *W* magazine if her husband was the love of her life, she responded, 'Is he the love of my life? I mean, I don't know. I've never been someone who says, "He's the love of my life." He's certainly a big love in my life.'

It is thought that, by this stage, Jen suspected that all was not well in her relationship and according to a friend she was 'insanely jealous of how close Brad and Ange were'.

Mr. & Mrs. Smith is about a married couple who

theoretically should be perfectly happy with their life but are bored of their relationship and, ironically, before filming had started Angelina had said of the story, 'It's about marriage, which is interesting because he [Brad] has a great one and I have had some bad experiences.'

This obviously all changed when Brad met Angelina and Jen began to feel that Brad was being distant; on one of the most emotional evenings of her life, the filming of the last-ever episode of *Friends* in January 2004 – her husband said he couldn't make it because of work commitments. Having worked on the show for ten years, Aniston viewed the cast and crew as her family and went through a grieving process when her Central Perk days came to an end. In an interview after her separation from Pitt, Aniston talked about how emotionally unavailable her husband had become and how he 'just wasn't there' for her any more.

According to her best friend and *Friends* co-star Courteney Cox Arquette, Brad was honest with Jen about the fact that he was developing feelings for Jolie, but tried to work through it and save his marriage. 'I don't think he started an affair physically, but I think he was attracted to her,' said Cox of Brad's relationship with Angelina. 'There was a connection and he was honest about that with Jen. Most of the time when people are attracted to other people, they don't tell. At least he was honest about it. It was an attraction he fought for a period of time.'

Another friend of the actress said, 'Brad was influenced by

Angelina – particularly her humanitarian efforts. He changed. Jennifer knew [Angelina] got under his skin and it bothered her.'

And James Cruse, a friend of Brad's, confirmed that Brad was smitten. 'I've never met anyone like her,' he told James. It's somehow ironic that Pitt should have been so impressed with Angelina's charity work and political views, given that years previously he had laughed at the idea that he should have a valid view on any such matters. 'Reporters ask me what I feel China should do about Tibet,' said Pitt. 'Who cares what I feel China should do about Tibet? I'm a fucking actor! They hand me a script. I act. Basically, when you whittle everything away, I'm a grown man who puts on make-up.'

Brad had obviously changed his tune by the time he met Angelina, but she insists that his change of heart was nothing to do with her influence. 'He never talked about politics or the charity things he's done, but I realised he was aware of these issues,' she told *Vogue*.

Brad was indeed a changed man, and his attraction to Angelina was obviously one that he couldn't fight forever. Despite being pictured on what appeared to be a romantic break in Anguilla with Jen (the couple were accompanied by Courteney Cox, her husband David Arquette and their daughter Coco) in January 2001, the couple announced their separation almost immediately afterwards. Given that just days earlier they had been snapped strolling along the beach arm in arm, stopping only to kiss, the world was more than a little shocked to hear the following announcement, which they made to *People* magazine: 'After seven years together, we have decided to formally separate. For those who follow these sorts of things, we want to explain our separation is not the result of speculation in the tabloid media. It's the result of much thoughtful consideration. We remain committed friends with great love and admiration for one another. We ask in advance for your kindness and sensitivity in coming months.'

According to Jen's friends, the actress very much saw this separation as a temporary measure and expected that, once they had worked through their problems, she and her husband would be reunited. 'They're still in love,' said one. 'They need to reconnect to who they were before they got married.'

This is not to say that Jen was kidding herself about the depth of her husband's feelings for another woman, but, given that Brad had absolutely insisted that he hadn't slept with Angelina, she thought there was a chance that after some time apart they could go back to being a couple.

According to Kristin Hahn, an executive at Pitt and Aniston's production company Plan B, 'She's not suggesting she didn't know there was an enchantment, and a friendship. But Brad was saying, "This is not about another woman."' Pitt had told Jen that he needed to figure himself out and, as much as she tried to convince him to do this while remaining married, he insisted that needed to do it without her.

Brad may have told his wife that their separation was nothing to do with another woman, but, when photographs of him and Angelina looking cosy on the set of *Mr. & Mrs. Smith* emerged at the end of January, things didn't look good for Jen. With Angelina pictured leaning on Brad's shoulder in a break between filming on the Amalfi Coast, near Naples, the picture implied a great deal of intimacy between the co-stars and didn't exactly send out a 'just good friends' message. Even after the pictures became public, the couple refused to admit that there was anything untoward going on between them and, in an interview in the March issue of *Vanity Fair*, Angelina was adamant that her feelings for Brad were not based on anything other than friendship but admitted, 'It's obviously been difficult with all this bullshit going on.' When asked about how she had heard about Brad and Jen splitting up, she said, 'When [Pitt and Aniston] separated, I was in Niger, in a place where there are no newspapers and nobody gossips.' And she certainly wasn't about to pass judgement on their relationship. 'I knew nothing about their marriage,' she said. 'All I know is they seem like wonderful people and wonderful friends and they seem like – I wish people could learn from them and how they obviously seem to be so close...'

There had been a rumour in the press that the final straw in the Pitt–Aniston marriage was when Jen overheard Brad and Angelina having phone sex, but the actress dismissed the claims as 'absolute bullshit' and also denied that she had ever said she had been 'a shoulder to cry on' for Brad. In fact, she was so angry about the latter statement that she actually sent word to Jen and Brad's agent that the story was entirely false and she had said no such thing. In her defence, Jolie also claimed that the picture of her and Brad looking close had been doctored to make it look like they were standing a lot nearer each other than they actually were.

For all her protestations, it was clear that Jolie had strong feelings for Pitt and, although they may not have consummated their relationship physically before his marriage had ended, the seed of love had certainly been sown. When asked about her experiences on the set of *Mr. & Mrs. Smith*, Angelina gushed about what a fantastic co-star Brad was and how 'funny' and 'goofy' he was and even went as far as to say that he was 'a great kisser' during their love scenes. 'He's wonderful. He's a great guy,' she said. 'He's really down to earth, he's really smart and he's a great actor. I mean, if I had to be trapped doing a film with anyone for as long as we've been doing this one, I'm glad it's him.'

Brad was equally taken with Jolie and defended her wild reputation, saying, 'I have never seen someone as misperceived as Angelina. She's surprisingly level headed, bright and incredibly decent.'

Never one to be backwards in coming forwards when it came to throwing herself into a relationship, the fact that Brad was still married may have been what held Angelina back from giving in to her feelings for him. Given that her own parents' relationship broke down due to her father's infidelities, Angelina maintained that getting involved with a married man was something she simply wouldn't do. 'To be intimate with a married man when my own father cheated on my mother is not something that I could forgive,' she said. 'I couldn't look at myself in the morning if I did that. It's not nice to be breaking up a marriage.'

One plucky tabloid reporter asked Angelina outright if she had slept with Brad on the set, only to be told, 'I did not shag Brad Pitt. No, absolutely not.'

If this is true – and even Aniston has said that she chooses to believe that Brad was faithful to her for the duration of their marriage – then it's easy to see why Angelina was so sick of all the marriage-wrecker accusations, but over the years she hadn't exactly done anything to play down her man-eater reputation and it was now coming back to haunt her. Although she was always happy to be open and honest in interviews, this resulted in her being labelled as a 'bad girl' as opposed to Jennifer Aniston's 'good girl' and this pigeonholing had started to take its toll. 'In this business, it's like: are you the funny person, are you the good girl, the bad girl, the homemaker? It seems impossible for people to absorb the fact that somebody could be sexual and wild and a bit dangerous – maybe to the point of stupidity – but also love being a mom and a person who has a conscience and is compassionate.'

This comment was obviously a response to the fact that, since one of the most shocking celeb break-ups of all time, the media had thrived on the thought of these two very different women thrashing it out over a man. Shops across America even started to produce Team Aniston and Team Jolie T-shirts so that the public could show where their sympathies lay – and, unsurprisingly, the Team Aniston T-shirts are said to have outsold the Team Jolie ones by 25 to 1. The media's interpretation of events was also something that greatly upset Jen and she clearly resented the fact that she had no control over her involvement in the love triangle. 'It was horrendous,' she reflected afterwards. 'When it was happening, I simply tuned out. There was a lot of toxic stuff out there and to be able to survive all that it was necessary to move through it as cleanly as I could and think positive.'

Jolie may not have enjoyed being seen as the 'bad girl' in the whole scenario, but, when pictures of her, Brad and Maddox playing on Diani Beach, Africa, were published on 29 April, there was little more the couple could do to deny the fact that they were an item. In the shots, Angelina looks on as Brad plays happily with her son and they look nothing short of the perfect family unit.

In the same *Vanity Fair* interview in which she denied any involvement with Pitt, Angelina said, 'I know if I ever saw a man be great with my child then that would be it for me. I actually know that.'

And here, for all the world to see, were pictures of Brad

being 'great' with her child. In fact, Maddox seems to have played a large part in their falling in love, given that Brad spent so much time with him between scenes on *Mr. & Mrs. Smith*. Much in the way that Colin Farrell had been mesmerised by Jolie's parenting skills, Brad was also said to be blown away by how fantastic she was with her son. Further reports from a source staying at the same African resort said the couple's lovemaking 'sounded like a wounded animal. Like someone being killed.' There were even suggestions that security guards were called to the scene for fear that there had been a terrible accident.

This evidence that her ex had already struck up a relationship with another woman was obviously a very bitter pill for Aniston to swallow and she admits that she was as flabbergasted with Brad's actions as anyone. 'The world was shocked and I was shocked. I'd be a robot if I said I didn't feel moments of anger, of hurt, of embarrassment,' she said. 'I can't say it was one of the highlights of my year. But shit happens.'

Jen not only had to deal with the fact that Brad had fallen in love with someone else, but also the speculation that the reason Brad left her was because she had refused to have his children. There had to be a reason for this seemingly perfect relationship to crumble and the general consensus was that Aniston had put her movie career before her relationship and Brad was fed up of waiting for her to settle down. Rumours abounded that he was desperately broody but that her ruthless ambition and determination to be remembered for something other than her alter ego Rachel Green was holding back his baby plans and nothing hurt Jen more than this. 'I don't want to be remembered for playing a fashionable airhead in *Friends*,' Jen was reported to have said. 'I want to make serious movies. No one remembers Robin Williams from *Mork and Mindy*.'

But, according to one of the couple's mutual friends, this notion that she was willing to put her career first was nonsense. 'When Brad and Jen were in the marriage, having a baby was not his priority ever,' said the friend. 'It was an abstract desire for him, whereas for Jen it was much more immediate.'

And Jen herself said that the rumours of her refusal to breed were a million miles from the truth. 'Do I want to have children? I do and I will,' she said. 'The women who inspire me are the ones who have families and children.' Jen not only felt that Brad could have spoken out to defend her on this topic and point out categorically that their separation was not down to her reluctance to get pregnant, but she also felt that the media would not have persecuted a man in such a fashion. 'A man divorcing would never be accused of choosing career over children,' said Jen. 'That really pissed me off. I've never in my life said I don't want to have children.' If anything, Jen felt that maybe it was her selfless nature which had caused the relationship to go wrong. 'I love taking care of people,' she said. 'And I definitely put his needs before mine sometimes.'

As if the pictures of Brad and Angelina in Africa weren't enough for Aniston to cope with, the actress was dealt another massive blow in the form of a magazine shoot that Angelina and Brad did together for *W* magazine. In the July issue, Brad and Angelina featured in a 60-page photoshoot that depicted married life in sixties America, entitled 'Domestic Bliss'. Brad and Angelina appeared as man and wife with a brood of miniature blond Brads posing as their children. Inspired by the unhappy marriage depicted in *Mr. & Mrs. Smith*, Brad came up with the concept of the shoot and with the help of photographer Steven Klein they created a photo essay that looked at a disillusioned married couple living in suburbia around the time of Kennedy's assassination in 1963, the year Brad was born. Brad said that, in keeping with the themes present in *Mr. & Mrs. Smith*, he wanted to explore the 'unidentifiable malaise' that wrecks many apparently perfect marriages. 'You don't know what's wrong,' he said, 'because the marriage is everything you signed up for.'

Given that he had just walked out of his own seemingly perfect marriage and chosen to do the shoot with the person he was being romantically linked to, this project, however artistic, was deemed incredibly insensitive on Brad's part. The parts he and Angelina were playing in the shoot may have been those of an unhappy couple, but it still seemed incredibly cruel to pour salt into Jen's wounds in such a fashion.

When asked about the shoot, Jen said simply, 'There's a sensitivity chip that's missing.'

A further blow to the actress was the fact that Brad not only came up with the idea himself but also retained international rights to the pictures and made money from them. In the words of Jen's friend Kristin Hahn, 'This woman is basically having a root canal without anaesthesia...'

W magazine aside, pictures of Brad, Angelina and Maddox continued to appear in magazines and newspapers across the globe and after their trip to Africa together they went on to visit countries such as Morocco and Ethiopia, the country from which Angelina would adopt her next child, Zahara Marley Jolie. Before the adoption, which took place on 6 July, Angelina and Brad attended the LA premiere of *Mr. & Mrs. Smith* on 7 June and, again, went to great lengths to dispel rumours that they were together. After arriving separately on the red carpet, the couple refused to be photographed next to each other and journalists were forewarned that they would not be answering any questions about their relationship. Anyone who saw the film would have their questions answered right there. There is undeniable chemistry between the actors and the couple positively smoulder on screen. And, when asked whether their chemistry was natural or fake, Angelina admitted that it had come very naturally.

On the same day as the première, Brad was interviewed on *Prime Time Live* with Diane Sawyer and, again, he was very non-committal about any developments in his personal life. Brad granted Sawyer the interview on the basis that he could promote his new film and talk about his recent trip to visit starving children in Africa (he went on missions to South Africa and Ethiopia after visiting Kenya with Jolie) – a trip undoubtedly inspired by his new girlfriend. Between video footage of him talking to African children and doing his bit for charity, Sawyer managed to squeeze in the odd question about his love life, but a well-prepared Brad managed to be suitably vague and even questioned the media interest in his love life. 'It's a strange focus, isn't it?' he said. 'That my relationships or relationship mishaps take precedence over something like that [the situation in Africa]... I understand it's about entertainment, but, man, it's misguided a bit, isn't it?' He went on to describe Jen as an 'extraordinary person', while Angelina Jolie was labelled 'a good egg'. As to whether this 'good egg' was his new girlfriend, Pitt would only go as far as to say, 'It's more that there's not so much to talk about at this time. There's a lot still to, I guess, put into place... Listen, I don't know what the future is just yet.'

Sawyer asked him directly if Jolie was the reason his marriage broke down, to which Brad responded, 'No, it's a good story.' He did admit, however, that his desire to have children hadn't been dampened by his forthcoming divorce (Aniston filed for divorce on 25 March, citing irreconcilable differences) and said, 'The dreams don't change. The dreams become more vivid.'

While the dreams had become more 'vivid' for Brad, Jen's had become a nightmare and the fact that Brad almost looked excited about the prospect of life without her must have been incredibly hard to swallow. 'It's a really interesting time,' he told Sawyer. 'It's a shake-up year... I make my choices and I live with those. I like that. My mistakes are my mistakes. My wins are my wins – that I can live with.'

The role of humanitarian was a new one for the actor, and cynics would say that his actions, while done with good intentions, were a result of his obsession with Jolie and an attempt to become embroiled in her world. Jolie defended Brad's efforts and claimed that there was a lot we didn't know about this man, who thus far had been best known more for his looks, his acting and his famous wife rather than his desire to put an end to world poverty. 'People know very little about him, I think, when it comes to where his morals are, where his values are, how he is with people, what he cares about, what he's learned about,' she said. 'And he's a very aware person. He's doing a lot of good things. And he's a great parent. And so certainly it's nice to watch him do that. And it's nice for me to be able to talk about the things I care about and with somebody that does as well.'

In a similar vein to Brad's interview with Sawyer, Jolie appeared on the *Today* show with Ann Curry on NBC but the actress who was previously renowned for being honest and gushing about her relationships clearly thought the better of it this time round. Curry pushed and pushed the actress to admit to what was going on, reasoning that if she just came clean then the fuss would die down, but Angelina wasn't budging. 'People will say what they want to say, and it's OK,' she told Curry. 'And my life will go on, and I need to focus on my life. So, do I need to defend that I'm a decent woman? I sure hope I don't. I know I am.' And, even when she did later talk about her feelings for Brad, it was still very undefined and evasive. 'I think the world of Brad,' she said. 'We did eventually become close – any couple working so intimately would. But I will tell you there was no bedroom action. But, yes, my feelings for him did escalate. And love? Well, what is that? I feel love for my little boy Maddox. And, yes, I suppose a different kind of love remains between me and Brad. What I will say is that we have grown very close.'

It wasn't until two years after they got together that Angelina finally admitted that the couple knew there was more to their relationship than just friendship when they were filming *Mr. and Mrs. Smith*. 'I think we were both the last two people looking for a relationship,' she told *Vogue*. 'I was quite content to be a single mom with Mad. And I didn't know much about exactly where Brad was in his personal life. But it was clear he was with his best friend, someone he loves and respects.' They may not have been looking for a relationship, but, as Jolie points out, their attraction was too strong to overlook. 'Because of the film, we ended up being brought together to do all these crazy things, and I think we found this strange friendship and partnership that just kind of suddenly happened. I think a few months in I realised, "God, I can't wait to get to work." Whether it was arguing about a scene or dance class or doing stunts – anything we had to do together – we just found a lot of joy in it together. We just kind of became a pair.'

Despite rumours that they acted on their feelings before Brad split with Jen, Angelina insists that it wasn't until filming had finished that they realised what was happening. 'It took really until the end of the shoot for us to realise that it might mean something more than we'd earlier allowed ourselves to believe. And both knowing that the reality of that was a big thing, something that was going to take a lot of serious consideration. We spent a lot of time contemplating and thinking and talking about what we both wanted in life and realised that we wanted very, very similar things. And then we just continued to take time. And then life developed in a way where we could be together, where it felt like something we would do, we *should* do.'

So, while Brad and Angelina, or 'Brangelina' as they were soon labelled, grew closer, Jen was left to lick her wounds and attempt to rebuild her life without her husband. And, while he jetted round the globe with his new girlfriend and her son, Brad was philosophical about his past. 'I know that, if a marriage doesn't fit a certain idea, it's looked upon as a failure,' he said. 'But I see mine as a total success. Jen is such an influence on my life. We made it for seven years – that's five years more than I made it with anyone else.'

While many other women in her position would have taken every opportunity to bad-mouth their ex and express the bitterness that she surely felt, Jen refused to give in to such temptation. She admitted that she had held 'pity parties' for herself, indulged in 'serious therapy sessions' and screamed at the water's edge of her Malibu home occasionally, but for the most part Jen remained as positive about the marriage as Brad did. 'I don't regret any of that time and I'm not here to beat myself up about it,' she said. 'They were seven very intense years together and it was a beautiful, complicated relationship. I love Brad; I really love him. He's a fantastic man. I will love him for the rest of my life and hope that some day we will be able to be friends again.'

chapter 16

a child is born

As the old saying goes, actions speak louder than words, and, despite the couple remaining tight-lipped for the first two years of their relationship, the love story of Brad and Angelina was told in pictures. They were photographed visiting Tokyo, Canada and Pakistan (where they spent Thanksgiving and viewed the impact of the 8 October Kashmir earthquake that killed almost 100,000 and left tens of thousands homeless), but the couple made the most important of their trips in July to Ethiopia. On 6 July, Brad, Angelina and Maddox visited the Horizons For Children orphanage in Addis Ababa and collected Angelina's second adopted child, Zahara Marley Jolie. Although Angelina had made no secret of her desire to adopt more children after Maddox, the actress had kept quiet about where exactly she planned to do it. Nine months prior to collecting her daughter, there had been reports of Jolie visiting an orphanage in Moscow (Moscow's Baby House Number 13) and it was thought that there she had fallen in love with a seven-month-old blond-haired blue-eyed boy called Gleb. Angelina said of these stories, 'I was going to adopt this other child in Russia, but it didn't work out, so I may adopt another in about six months. Maddox is three years old now and I don't think he's quite ready for a sibling just yet.'

Maddox may well have been one of the reasons that the adoption of Gleb didn't work out, but there was also a growing unease in Russia regarding foreign adoptions and it's thought that this could also have been a contributing factor. Luckily for Zahara, an AIDS orphan (born Tena Adam on 8 January 2005) whose mother died at the age of 22 and whose father is unknown, Angelina's attentions turned to Ethiopia after encountering problems in Russia. As was the case with Maddox, Jolie fell in love at first sight and she knew Zahara, who was living in a one-room shack with no electricity with her maternal grandmother and two aunts, was the child she wanted to take home with her. The name 'Zahara' is of Hebrew origin and means 'flower', while 'Marley' was bestowed on her after the late Jamaican reggae star Bob Marley. Jolie would later go on to call her daughter 'Z' for short.

The fact that Brad accompanied Angelina on such a significant day of her – and Maddox's – life was evidence enough that these two were planning a long-term future together, even if they struggled to come to terms with their new relationship. 'We were so used to not being together when I was adopting Zahara and going through the follow-up home study, the woman said, "How long have you been together? And can you explain your relationship?" And she's obviously not a reporter. She's just a woman doing her job. But we both got hysterical. We couldn't answer the questions. We were like two idiots. "What do you mean? We're not... We've never had a..." We're like two great friends and if we talk about the relationship seriously it just seems odd. I mean, on occasion, we are obviously very capable of being serious with each other.'

Hysteria aside, Angelina had always made it clear that anyone she became involved with would have to understand her desire to adopt, saying, 'If I meet a man and we want to settle down together, I would hope he'd love my son like a blood child and understand adoption.'

Sure enough, six months after she'd adopted Zahara, Brad proved to her that he not only understood adoption but also wanted to be part of it. In December 2005, it was announced that Pitt was formally adopting Maddox and Zahara and, with the approval of a California judge, their names would be legally changed to Jolie-Pitt. Although, according to Angelina, Maddox had viewed Brad as a father figure long before he was legally adopted by him. 'He just out of the blue called him Dad,' she told *Vogue*. 'It was amazing. We were playing with cars on the floor of a hotel room, and we both heard it and didn't say anything and just looked at each other. And then we just kind of let it go on... that was probably the most defining moment, when he decided that we would all be a family.'

Although Angelina was delighted to bring Zahara back to the States with her, it wasn't long before her six-month-old daughter became a cause for concern. Shortly after arriving in the States, Angelina realised that something was wrong but put it down to the fact that Zahara wasn't drinking enough formula. Jolie stated that 'she was six months and not nine pounds. Her skin, you could squeeze it, it stuck together.'

Jolie consulted doctors and her daughter was immediately admitted to the emergency room at New York Presbyterian Hospital, where she was treated for dehydration, malnutrition and a salmonella infection for a week. Like the doting mother that she is, Angelina stayed by her daughter's side night and day (Brad himself was in a different hospital at the time suffering with viral meningitis) and waited anxiously for little Zahara to put on weight and recover. According to paediatrician Jane Aronson, who nursed Zahara through her illness, the baby had gone 'from the depression of abandonment [after the death of her birth mother] to being completely and unconditionally loved and attached'. She also commented on the close bond between mother and daughter, saying, 'Zahara is completely connected to Angelina. They are one, They're in love.'

Much to Jolie's relief, it wasn't long before Zahara was on the mend and she put on so much weight that Brad and Angelina affectionately nicknamed her 'chubby'.

Unfortunately, it wasn't only Zahara's health that caused Angelina problems, as soon after the adoption news reports emerged in which several women claimed to be Zahara's birth mother or grandmother. This was very similar to the predicament Jolie had found herself in with Maddox and, again, she had to endure lots of speculation about whether the adoption of Zahara was entirely legitimate. By declaring Zahara to be an AIDS orphan, Angelina had made it clear to the world that her birth mother was dead, but this did not put a stop to the media frenzy surrounding her daughter's heritage. Jolie also had to put up with Zahara's grandmother's claims that Zahara was taken from her without permission, but, in late October 2005, an Ethiopian judge ruled that there was no evidence to suggest that Jolie would have to file for re-adoption of her daughter. The judge also ruled that one particular woman who said she was Zahara's birth mother was making false claims.

Throughout all this turmoil, Brad was a constant presence by Angelina's side despite working on two movies at the time, *Babel* and *The Assassination Of Jesse James By The Coward Robert Ford*, and he was often pictured playing the doting dad, carrying Maddox in one arm and Zahara in the other, in between breaks. If anyone ever doubted that he was a hands-on dad, one particularly touching picture of him holding Zahara with a baby bottle hanging out of his jeans pocket proved to the world where his priorities lay.

Shortly after adopting Zahara, Angelina too was back on a film set, this time for *The Good Shepherd*, which told the story of the birth of the CIA and was directed by (as well as starring) Robert De Niro. This film, which also stars Matt Damon and Joe Pesci, was shot in the Dominican Republic and it was at this time that rumours of Jolie's pregnancy started circulating. Ever since she and Brad had got together, the media had been speculating about when they would try for a baby and subsequent paparazzi shots taken of Angelina in loose clothing only added fuel to the fire. It was while chatting to a charity worker in Santa Domingo in Dominican Republic that the actress confirmed, 'Yes, I am pregnant,' and within two days of making this statement an official announcement came from Brad's Pitt's publicist Cindy Guagenti. On 12 January, just over a year after Brad's separation from Jen, Guagenti declared, 'I can confirm they are expecting. There isn't a lot more to say.'

Again, the couple let pictures of them do the talking and, at the end of January, on a trip to Haiti, they posed for photos and, clad in a tight T-shirt and jeans, Angelina's substantial bump was there for all the world to see. The couple made this particular trip to visit a school in Port-au-Prince supported by Yele Haiti for the first anniversary of the charity founded by Haitian-born hip-hop musician

Wyclef Jean, and Angelina had arranged a deal with *People* magazine allowing them to print the first picture of her pregnant in exchange for a $500,000 donation to the charity. Half a million dollars may have seemed like a hefty fee, but for *People* magazine the pictures were worth every penny. Gazing into each other's eyes, the couple seemed to be blissfully in love; these were the shots the world had been waiting to see. Angelina knew she could negotiate a ludicrous fee for such pictures and, yet again, used her pulling power to raise awareness for a cause she cared about deeply. She had always liked to juggle several things at the same time in her life but it turned out that adopting a new baby, working on a film, falling pregnant and doing charity work proved to be a bit much for the actress and Brad had great cause for concern when she collapsed on the set of *The Good Shepherd* after suffering from exhaustion. Concerned doctors put her on high-risk pregnancy alert and Jolie, who was alarmingly slim in every area other than her bump, was told to cut back her gruelling schedule. Fortunately for the actress, *The Good Shepherd* was the only film she'd signed up for before realising she was pregnant and once filming was over she would take it easy and prepare herself for her first natural birth.

While Angelina and Brad were positively ecstatic about their pregnancy, there was one person who didn't take the pregnancy news so well. When Brad split with Jen, her friend Kristin Hahn said, 'My worst fear is that Jen will have to face them having a baby soon, because that would be beyond painful.'

Jen herself had broken down during an interview for *Vanity Fair* when the journalist merely brought up the rumours of Angelina's pregnancy. 'She looks as if I've stabbed her in the heart. Her eyes well up and spill over,' wrote the reporter.

Not only were Jen's worst fears confirmed, but it is thought that Brad couldn't face telling his ex the news personally and so Aniston found out with the rest of the world. As devastated as she was, Jen told a friend, 'The nauseous feeling I expected to have when I heard the news is smaller than I thought.'

Regardless of his ex-wife's feelings, Brad was no longer in a place where he wanted to hide his love for Angelina and he told a friend, James Cruse, that he was fed up of playing his feelings down. 'We're so happy,' he told James. 'We're sort of tired of playing cat-and-mouse games about our relationship. Angie and I love each other so much. We're crazy about each other and we want to shout it from the rooftops.'

Many sceptics had assumed that as soon as the lust faded between Pitt and Jolie their relationship would falter, but, on the contrary, the attachment between them seemed to grow and grow. 'Not only is she hot, but she cares deeply about others,' Brad told a friend. 'I've never known anyone so compassionate. She's made me stop and think about what's important in life, and it's not making movies or having your picture in magazines.'

And Cruse admitted that, since hooking up with Jolie, Brad had become almost unrecognisable. 'He's a totally different man than he was when he was with Jennifer,' reflected Cruse.

For mutual friends of Brad and Jen, it was difficult to play fair to both sides, but no one could deny Brad's obvious happiness. George Clooney, who became close to Brad and subsequently Jen when the actors worked together on the *Ocean's 11* and *Ocean's 12* movies, said, 'Brad's break-up with Jennifer really saddened me but I've met Angelina a few times. She is a very beautiful woman and very clued up. I'm happy if Brad is happy. I see them together and they look very content.'

Brad's parents Bill and Jane, who were also very close to their former daughter-in-law, were initially distraught when he decided to leave Jen, but after meeting Angelina it's believed that Bill looked at Brad and said, 'You've made the right choice, son.'

Brad's gran Betty Russell also approved of her grandson's new love: 'Now he's got Angelina, he seems really happy,' she said. 'He'll make a great dad, he's very much a family man.'

Even Jon Voight, who hadn't met Brad or spoken to his daughter for years, described them as a 'great match'.

As the birth of her baby drew closer, Angelina may have

stopped making films but she was still determined to continue her humanitarian work and once again she used her celebrity status to raise awareness of a matter close to her heart. Jolie agreed to another interview with Ann Curry for *NBC News* in April, but this time it was to take place in Namibia, where she, Brad and the kids were taking a holiday. Curry travelled to Namibia and spoke to the actress about her latest mission, to improve the lot of 100 million children across the planet who can't go to school because of war, lack of opportunity or because they're poverty stricken. The ultimate goal of the global education drive is that, by the year 2015, children everywhere should complete at least a fifth-grade education. This was a cause particularly close to the actress's heart, given that Zahara could easily have been one of the kids who grew up without an education. 'She's from a country where six million kids don't go to school every year... Her mother died of AIDS and they wouldn't have had any funds to send her to school,' explained Jolie. 'I just think, especially my daughter, there's no possible way she would have gone to school. She is so smart and so strong. And her potential as a woman one day is great.' Jolie had always maintained that Maddox would grow up aware of his Cambodian roots and similarly, with Zahara, she hoped that she would grow up with an affinity to her birth country. 'Hopefully, she will be active in her country and in her continent when she's older. And. because she'll have a good education, she'll be able to do that much more.

Curry obviously wasn't going to let the actress escape without asking questions about Brad and her pregnancy. Angelina by this time (the interview took place at the end of April) was sporting a huge bump and admitted that, although she'd had a 'very fortunate pregnancy' with no morning sickness, her hormones had caused her to become a bit 'hysterical'. 'Apparently that's what I've gotten from pregnancy,' she admitted. 'Brad said this to me, too. I get hysterical now. Like, hysterical to the point of crying and falling off the bed... Like, I'll try to read, and then I'll start laughing. It'll last for, like, 20 minutes. And then, you know, I'll sit back down and focus again. He's reading, and I'm reading. And we're sitting there really serious... and then I'll just go. Like, it'll go on for – for hours. [Laughter] It's really horrible.'

A glowing Angelina also admitted, 'I have a lot to be happy about,' but rather naively insisted that she and Brad still didn't realise why there was so much fuss surrounding their relationship, saying that they thought it was 'just kind of funny'. The giggling actress, who admitted they knew the sex of their baby but refused to divulge the information, said, 'If he [Brad] saw this, he would probably understand why I was laughing. Because I just don't know how to address that kind of thing.' She added, 'I don't talk about our relationship in public. But we also don't talk about it at home... It's one of those funny things that just happens, and you live your life, and you're a family. But you never actually discuss [it].'

Given that the actress had always been adamant that she would never give birth to a child and only adopt, Curry asked her what had changed her mind, only to be told by Jolie that she still couldn't quite believe she was having a child naturally. 'I'm still kind of in denial about it. I still have this kind of funny thing of, like, "I can't quite believe it." I was always very sure that I'd adopt all my children. And I was quite at peace with that. And then things felt different... We'll continue to adopt. But now I'm pregnant.' It was typical of Angelina to talk about future adoptions when she hadn't even given birth yet, but Jolie pointed out that she and Pitt were in a privileged position, which meant they could afford help. 'We love children, you know?' she told Curry. 'And, fortunately, we have the resources to be able to get help where we need it. So I think there's no real plan about stopping. There's just talk about lots of them.'

Given her affection for Africa and its people, it was no surprise that the unconventional Jolie decided that she wanted to give birth in Namibia and two months before the baby was due she set up camp there with Brad, Maddox and Zahara in tow. Most Hollywood actresses would balk at the idea of giving birth in a Third World country, but Angelina wanted to get away from the media frenzy that surrounded her and Brad in the States and felt that Africa was the perfect place for her to have a quiet, peaceful birth. She was obviously aware that she would have access to much more sophisticated medical care in the States, but, if the doctors there were good enough for the people of Namibia, then they were good enough for her. It's thought that Brad was initially reluctant to go along with the idea and was concerned that in the event of any complications his partner would not have access to the help she needed, but there was no talking her round. While Aniston claimed that she felt that at times she put Pitt's feelings before her own in their marriage, there was no doubt that Jolie wore the trousers in this relationship. She was no less headstrong now than she was as a rebellious teenager, and once she had her heart set on it there was little anyone could do to change her mind. Having the baby in Africa also meant that there was lots of time for Brad's Malibu mansion to be remodelled while they were gone. Brad had bought this particular house before he married Jen and it was something of a bachelor pad, which wasn't exactly ideal to raise kids in. As soon as he split from Jen, he moved back into the house and, after he promised to make it more child-friendly, Angelina agreed to move the family in.

En route to Namibia, the Jolie-Pitts had an extended stay in Paris, where Angelina's mother, who had been diagnosed with ovarian cancer seven years earlier, was staying. Again, Angelina was adamant that they should shun the luxury abode they could certainly afford and insisted that they stayed in a very basic tower block. Brad was happy to be in Paris as it was a chance for him to get to know Marcheline, whom Angelina was incredibly close to, but, again, he was frustrated at his girlfriend's choice of accommodation. Jolie's argument was that if they stayed out of the limelight then there was less chance of disruption and she could get on with spending quality time with her mother out of the public eye. At one point, Jolie even considered giving birth in France so she could have her beloved mother by her side, but in the end the lure of Namibia was too strong.

Before arriving at the Burning Shore resort, where the family would stay until the birth, Angelina and Brad booked all seven rooms and five suites for two months at the cost of £185,000 to ensure their privacy. Although the main objective was to relax and prepare for the new arrival, Jolie and Pitt took time out to get to know the locals and had powerful help protecting their privacy from the government of Namibia, which refused to grant entry to reporters seeking to cover the birth without the actors' written permission. The government arrested photographers, confiscated film, ringed the couple's hotel with heavy security and set up large green barriers on the beach to shield the family, and their efforts were greatly appreciated by the A-list stars. One person who was allowed access to the country was James Haven, Angelina's much-loved brother, whom she wanted to be there for this landmark moment in her life. Despite plans to give birth naturally in the resort, the baby was in the breech position, which meant that Angelina had to be taken to the Cottage Medi-Clinic Hospital in Swakopmund, Namibia, for an emergency caesarean section. The caesarean went without a hitch and on 27 May Angelina gave birth to daughter Shiloh Nouvel Jolie-Pitt. Jason Rothbart, the couple's obstetrician, who had flown in from LA for the birth, gave the following statement:

Angelina underwent a scheduled caesarean due to breech presentation. The baby was a healthy seven pounds. Brad was with Angelina in the operating room the entire time and cut the umbilical cord of his daughter. The surgery and birth went flawlessly.

The birth of Brad and Angelina's baby was the most anticipated celebrity event in years (at just eight weeks old, Shiloh was to be immortalised in wax by Madame Tussauds in New York), and as soon as the statement was released people were rushing to find out the meaning of their daughter's name. They might not be one to favour many celebrity trends, but Brangelina certainly didn't let the side down when it came to picking an unusual name. By naming her Shiloh Nouvel, Brad and Angelina managed to combine the old with the new, for Shiloh is Hebrew in origin and means 'peaceful one' or 'His gift' and Nouvel means 'new' in French. Given that Angelina herself had a French middle name in the form of 'Jolie', it's thought she may have been keen to make this inclusion something of a family tradition. There was a lot of speculation at one stage that the child would be given a Namibian name, but in the event this turned out to be just another rumour.

Given that they had travelled all the way to Africa to ensure their privacy for the birth, it was expected that the tight-lipped couple would say little to the public regarding their bundle of joy, but, like most new parents, both Pitt and Jolie were so overwhelmed with happiness that they couldn't keep quiet. 'It's the most amazing thing that's ever happened to us,' said Jolie following the birth, while an equally ecstatic Brad gushed, 'It was an amazing, beautiful, spiritual moment when our daughter Shiloh was born. Angelina was incredible and I feel very blessed. Our daughter is the most beautiful, precious thing.'

Jolie's brother James also described the emotions he felt when he saw his niece for the first time: 'I walked in the room and it was so overwhelming I had to walk out. To see the father, mother, daughter – it was such a beautiful image that it overtook me. I've never seen her [Angelina] happier.'

He had been left in charge of Maddox and Zahara and took them along to see their younger sister. While Maddox described her as 'beautiful', Zahara, who was only 18 months old, wasn't quite as enamoured by the new addition to the family. 'Z's a little jealous because [Shiloh's] a girl,' admitted Jolie. 'But Maddox loves her. It's like having a pet he can hold and look at. I was kind of prepared to defend my other children. I was prepared to give them extra love and attention because something was going to be different about this one.'

In fact, in an interview six months after the birth, Jolie

aired the controversial view that she actually had stronger feelings for her adopted children than she did for Shiloh. She told *Elle* magazine, 'The world has this opinion about the difference, then you wonder if there [is] a difference. In fact, I found the opposite. I feel so much more for Mad and Z because they are survivors, they came through so much. Shiloh seemed so privileged from the moment she was born, I have less inclination to feel for her. I met my other kids when they were six months, they came with a personality. A newborn really is this... blob! I'm conscious to make sure I don't ignore her needs, just because I think the others are more vulnerable.'

Marcheline may not have present for her granddaughter's birth, but this didn't put a dampener on the momentous occasion and she declared, 'My heart is overflowing with joy with the new arrival of Brad and Angelina's third child. Maddox, Zahara and Shiloh are deeply loved children. They have very kind and caring parents who love and support each other in every way.'

While Pitt's parents flew over to Namibia to get a glimpse of Shiloh, Jon Voight could only communicate his good wishes to Angelina via the media, saying, 'I'm just so very happy for both of them. I'm almost unable to explain how deeply happy I am for her [Shiloh's] parents and so happy to have this new little one in the world.'

The birth may have gone relatively smoothly, but Jolie admitted afterwards that giving birth was a far more stressful experience than she had imagined. 'I was sure everything was going to go right and then at the last minute I became the mom who was sure everything was going to go wrong. 'You're just suddenly terrified that they're not gonna take a first breath. That was my whole focus. I just wanted to hear her cry.'

As a thank you to the people of Namibia for their kind hospitality, Jolie and Pitt gave a TV interview to rave about the treatment they had received and their love for the country. 'They've been so gracious and made our stay here very special,' Pitt told the Namibian Broadcasting Corporation.

'People were shocked that we chose to come here, and they thought we were putting our child's life in danger,' said Jolie. 'But we did our homework about Namibia. We want to tell the world how magnificent this country and the people are. We could not have received better medical healthcare in America.'

The general consensus was that the Hollywood couple had been very welcome guests (apart from a few reports which speculated that certain charity campaigners criticised them for exercising their power in the country) and Namibia's Environment and Tourism Deputy Minister, Leon Jooste, reinforced this when he said, 'Shiloh Nouvel Jolie-Pitt will be allowed to obtain Namibian citizenship, if the parents should choose to do so.'

After a two-month stay, Brad and Angelina left Namibia on 11 June leaving a $300,000 donation to the maternity ward Angelina had stayed in, and promised to return to the country they had grown so attached to, saying, 'We are proud our daughter was born here and we leave with fond memories and a hunger to return.'

On their return to the States, the couple unsurprisingly found that pictures of their newborn baby were in incredibly high demand and, once again, they decided to give the media what they wanted on the condition that lots of money would be donated to an undisclosed charity. There was a huge bidding war to get the first shots of baby Shiloh and eventually *People* magazine obtained the North American rights for $4.1 million, while *Hello!* magazine are rumoured to have paid $3.5 million for pictures. They may have been pricey, but the pictures certainly lived up to expectations, and Shiloh Nouvel was just as beautiful as the product of Brad Pitt and Angelina Jolie should be. With her dark hair, perfect pout and button nose, she really did look like 'the peaceful one' as her parents held her in their arms and posed for the cameras. Both Brad and Angelina looked mesmerised by her in every shot and Brad clearly hadn't been lying when he told Diane Sawyer in an interview in 2004, '[Little girls] They just crush me... they break my heart.'

Since getting together, Brad and Angelina had come a long way, and this latest juncture in Pitt's life could not have made him happier. He had gone from being in an unhappy marriage to being a loving, committed father of three in the space of 18 months and it was clear that meeting Angelina was the best thing that had ever happened to him. 'You know, I've had my day,' he said. 'Having children takes the focus off yourself, which I'm really grateful for. It's absolutely sublime. Whether you have them or adopt them, they're all blood. I'm so tired of thinking about myself. It's a true joy and a very profound love... having kids is the most extraordinary thing I've ever taken on.'

chapter 17

brad, babies and beyond

After the birth of Shiloh, the question on everyone's lips was if and when Brad and Angelina were going to take their relationship to the next level and get married, but so far the couple have seemed reluctant to take the plunge. There are several theories as to why this is the case, one being that, despite Brad's pleas, Angelina is reluctant to tie the knot again after two failed marriages. According to Brad's grandmother, Betty Russell, it is Pitt who is holding proceedings back due to residual feelings of guilt he carries from his marriage to Jen. 'Brad promised his last wife on their wedding day that they'd be together forever and they didn't make it. He is a sensitive soul who just wants to make sure he can keep his promise this time round.'

Angelina also appeared to be underwhelmed by the idea, and said, 'There is nothing in the air. We'll never marry. The focus is the kids and we are obviously extremely committed to the children and as parents together... to have a ceremony on top of it is nothing. We are legally bound to the children, not to each other, and I think that's the most important thing.' She did suggest, however, that, in spite of what Brad's grandmother had to say on the subject, he was keener on the idea than she was. 'If the kids get older and demand a ceremony, we might. It's a touchy subject,' she admitted.

Brad himself has said very little on the subject, but did say that he'd consider marrying Angelina when gay weddings became legal in the States. 'Angie and I will consider tying the knot when everyone else in the country who wants to be married is legally able.'

Despite their protestations, one very significant incident in Angelina's life may have changed all her ideas about marriage, that being the death of her much adored mother Marcheline. After battling ovarian cancer for seven years, Marceline Bertrand finally lost her fight on 27 January 2007 at the age of 56, and Angelina rushed to her side in the Cedars-Sinai Hospital in LA with Brad just three hours before her mother passed away. While her passing may not have come as a great shock to the actress, given the length of her illness, she was understandably distraught to lose the parent who she had been so close to her whole life. In a joint statement she released with her brother James Haven, Jolie said, 'There are no words to express what an amazing woman and mother she was. She was our best friend.'

In an interview in 2006, Jolie had heaped praise on Marcheline, saying, 'She raised us – and helped us become our own people. We are very much her life and I think we help her feel complete.'

According to reports, one of her mother's final comments to Angelina was: 'Marry that man', and it's thought that her mum's dying wish has had something of an impact on Angeline. A close friend of the family said, 'Marcheline held Angie's hand and told her, "You marry that man. He's an angel sent to look after you."' The friend also added, 'She asked Brad to look after Angelina and the children. Then she looked her daughter in the eyes and repeated what she'd been saying over and over to her for months.'

Angelina was said to be 'utterly choked' by her mum's request, and Brad, who had become very close to Marcheline since getting together with her daughter, is also said to have taken her wishes very seriously. 'Brad has never stopped trying to push her down the aisle but she's always resisted,' said the friend. 'Now she'll make good on her death-bed promise. I think she always had a little dream that, if she did wed Brad, it would be Marcheline who would give her away. Sadly, that can't be. But it shows how close she and Brad are, that Marcheline almost looked upon him as a son. She thought the world of him."

According to a close friend of Jolie's, Marcheline's death

has also highlighted the gap that the estrangement from her father has left in her life. 'Marcheline's death has done nothing to heal the rift between Angie and her father. She's never forgiven him for abandoning them and I believe she will take that resentment to her own grave. She was dreading this moment. She felt she had already lost her father – and now her mom too.'

Perhaps it will be the case that with her mother gone, Angelina will now crave the stability that marriage to Brad would give her, or perhaps she will remain true to her word and avoid any kind of formal commitment to the man that she loves. Either way, as their relationship has developed, the couple have discovered it's not just marriage they have a different attitude towards, with Brad wanting to settle down full time in their Malibu home and Angelina keen still to spread her wings and travel the world over. While Brad is something of a homebody, Angelina is determined that her kids will grow up as 'citizens of the world'. 'We'd like to have a base in the States. I'd like to have a base somewhere else too,' she said. 'I'd love to send the kids to international school and live in the middle of nowhere in Africa or Asia, just coming in [to the States] for work.'

Brad is also said to be reluctant to adopt another child so soon after the birth of Shiloh, but, unperturbed by the stress this could add to their lives, Angelina is keen to offer another baby a home as soon as possible. All she needs to do first is decide where she will go to find her next child. 'Next, we'll adopt,' she said. 'We don't know what country. It's gonna be the balance of what's right for Maddox and Z right now. It's, you know, another boy, another girl, which country, which race would fit in best with the kids.' Although she had a fairly easy pregnancy with Shiloh, Jolie has also admitted that she can't imagine giving birth to the number of children she would like. When asked how many she would like she said, 'Thirteen. But I sure as hell ain't squeezing all those out!'

Perhaps one of the other reasons Jolie is keen to adopt, as opposed to having another child biologically, is that, after the birth of Shiloh, the actress suffered from post-natal depression. Not only was she juggling the needs of three young children, but Jolie was also dealing with the stress of her mother's ongoing illness and it all proved a bit much for the normally resilient actress. In one interview she did shortly after giving birth, she said, 'Even just today I was breastfeeding and feeling tired. I don't know how I am going to get myself together again.'

Any surplus baby weight Jolie may have been carrying fast disappeared and these days there is little left of her curves. It can't have helped that, only two months after Shiloh was born, Brad was due back at work to make *Ocean's 13* with his old friend George Clooney. Angelina has always prided herself on being an incredibly independent woman, but she was reportedly annoyed at the amount of time Brad spent hanging out with his cast mates when she needed help at home. As one of the world's most famous bachelors, George Clooney was thought to have been a bad influence on Brad, and Angelina was angered by their partying antics.

The couple have now struck up a bargain, which means that neither of them will be absent from family life for too long at a time. 'Brad and I are only planning on doing one project a year so we can put all our time into the kids.'

After Pitt had finished making *Ocean's 13*, Jolie got straight back to work for a film produced by Brad and his ex-wife Jen's production company Plan B. *A Mighty Heart* is the true-life tale of Daniel Pearl, the investigative journalist who was kidnapped and subsequently murdered in Pakistan in 2002. Angelina plays Daniel's wife, Mariane Pearl, and the news that Jolie had taken on the role sparked controversy for two reasons. Firstly, Jennifer Aniston had originally planned to play Mariane but was dropped after her split from Brad; secondly, certain black campaign groups thought it was thought to be inappropriate for Angelina to play someone who is mixed race. Controversy aside, Jolie jumped at the chance of the part, because, as well as the subject matter being close to her heart, it also meant that, along with Brad and the kids, she could spend a great deal of time in India (filming didn't take place in Pakistan due to security fears).

Jolie may have put her heart and soul into her portrayal of Mariane, but it's clear that the joy of motherhood and finding Brad, the man she could share all her hopes and dreams with, has dampened her ambition and made her realise that there are more important things in life than work. 'I just don't care as much as I used to,' she admitted. 'I'm happier doing other things.'

The Angelina we know now is a much calmer, wiser and serene version of the one who burst on to the Hollywood scene all those years ago, and it appears that all her feelings of discontentment and disillusion with the world are now nothing but a distant memory. With Brad, she has found both stability and excitement, a best friend and a lover, and someone who looks like he's in it for the long haul. Before she met Brad, she said that the biggest problem in all her relationships had been that her partners never really understood her, saying, 'I've been loved, had fun and been inspired, but I've never had somebody whose way of thinking is similar to mine. Somebody to see all the things about me that I like about myself.'

In Brad, she had found a soulmate and someone who understood her need for rebellion and didn't run away from it or try to cage her in. He admired her humanitarian work, he was in awe of her skills as a mother and he understood that her lifestyle choices were never going to be conventional.

One of her *Tomb Raider* colleagues once said of Angelina, 'She is most definitely not normal and that's one of the most appealing things about her. I think it takes someone pretty special as a partner to be able to deal with that.'

275

Brad had proved himself to be this 'special partner', and Angelina knew how lucky she was to have found him. 'He's romantic, he makes time for us to talk, he's considerate, and he's great with the kids,' she said. 'What more could a girl ask for?'

filmography

Lookin' to Get Out (1982) ... Tosh

Cyborg 2 (1993) ... Casella 'Cash' Reese

Angela & Viril (1993) ... Angela

Alice & Viril (1993) ... Alice

Without Evidence (1995) ... Jodie Swearingen

Hackers (1995) ... Kate Libby/'Acid Burn'

Mojave Moon (1996) ... Eleanor 'Elie' Rigby

Love is All There is (1996) ... Gina Malacici

Foxfire (1996) ... Margret 'Legs' Sadovsky

True Women (1997) (TV) ... Georgia Virginia
   Lawshe Woods

George Wallace (1997) (TV) ... Cornelia Wallace

Playing God (1997) ... Claire

Gia (1998) (TV) ... Gia Marie Carangi

Hell's Kitchen (1998) ... Gloria McNeary

Playing by Heart (1998) ... Joan
Pushing Tin (1999) ... Mary Bell
The Bone Collector (1999) ... Amelia Donaghy
Girl, Interrupted (1999) ... Lisa Rowe
Gone in 60 Seconds (2000) ... Sara 'Sway' Wayland
Lara Croft: Tomb Raider (2001) ... Lara Croft
Original Sin (2001) ... Julia Russell/Bonnie Castle
Life or Something Like it (2002) ... Lanie Kerrigan
*Lara Croft Tomb Raider: The Cradle of
  Life* (2003) ... Lara Croft
Beyond Borders (2003) ... Sarah Jordan
Taking Lives (2004) ... Illeana
Shark Tale (2004) (voice) ... Lola
Sky Captain and the World of Tomorrow
  (2004) ... Franky
The Fever (2004) ... Revolutionary
Alexander (2004) ... Olympias
Mr. & Mrs. Smith (2005) ... Jane Smith
The Good Shepherd (2006) ... Clover Wilson
Beowulf (2007) ... Grendel's Mother
A Mighty Heart (2007) ... Mariane Pearl

bibliography

Angelina Jolie: Angel in Disguise – Edgar McFay
(2005, Icon Press)
Notes from My Travels – Angelina Jolie (2003,
Pocket Books)
*Brad & Jen: The Rise and Fall of Hollywood's
Golden Couple* – Mara Reinstein and Joey Bartolomeo
(2005, Wenner Media)